GW00802069

FUNNY THINGS HAPPENED TO ME ON

THE WAY TO OLD AGE

DAPHNE FARROW

To Dame Vera

Second edition

With enduring thanks

Daphne Farrow

Dedication

This book is dedicated to my daughters, Annie and Lesley, who have contributed to the recalling of these memories and without whose constant help and enthusiasm it would never have been finished.

Acknowledgements

My thanks go to Group Captain North for reading and correcting the text, The Ministry of Defence for their encouragement and help in providing photographs of World War II aircraft and to Margaret Lloyd for drawing the map of Gilfachwen Water.

Contents

Preface

So many funny things have happened to me during my long life and when I recount them there is always laughter. In writing this book I had the idea of spreading this laughter much further afield, as it is in rather short supply during these difficult times.

Through largely funny anecdotes, I record a selection of events in my life from 1921. An overview of some of the changes in lifestyle and attitudes in the UK, incidentally emerges through stories of my childhood, my father's involvement with William Morris in the development of the first Morris car, my youth, Plymouth Blitz, service in the WAAF in World War II, romance and marriage to a loving, courageous, RAF test pilot.

The book also covers raising children (the first one successfully delivered in the back of a taxi cab), post-war life in Bristol and a home help who was Mrs. Malaprop incarnate and stayed with us for fifteen splendid years.

Other moments of laughter come through stories of dogs, fly-fishing, holidays and a twenty-five year love affair with beautiful West Wales.

Although not every anecdote is strictly humorous, one of the many other definitions of funny – strange, bizarre, unusual - can almost certainly be applied.

Enjoy!

Chapter One

The early years

First appearance 7 November 1921

My mother always said that I cried incessantly for the first six months after my arrival and I'm really not surprised, as I didn't know where I was and I felt as if I had not only got on the wrong train but also had got out at the wrong station!

Right at the start, I found myself on the lap of a young man, who was running his hands up and down my body and poking things in my throat and nose.

I tried to assess where I was and, looking up, saw a large bed, where a dark-haired woman looked down at me with mild interest but without lifting a finger to rescue me. So I yelled and yelled. And that is where all the unfettered vocalisation started.

Six Months later

One day, I watched my mother open a tiny square parcel, take out the contents and pop it into her mouth. I was struck by the immediate alteration to her exhausted-looking features, due to her six months endurance test since I was born. A broad smile spread slowly across her lovely face, she closed her eyes and started chewing. I was astonished that something so small could create such a transformation. Then, to my surprise, she repeated the process and popped another toffee into her mouth, the stress and strain on her face completely disappearing like pure magic – abracadabra!

By this time, I was thinking that if the small, paper-wrapped parcels could create such a splendid effect on my mother, what then could they do for me?

As I watched, I started to dribble and this caught my mother's eye; at once the message was received and understood. She unwrapped a toffee for me, held it to my lips to lick.....and I grew up to be a happy child. The magic of Tucker's Toffee.

My mother

My mother, May Lilian Keeler, was born in Oxford in 1897, the ninth of ten children. For some of them, their playmate was Alice Liddell, the subject of Alice in Wonderland, the author being their local curate, better known as Lewis Carroll.

Mother was fair-skinned, dark-haired, blue-eyed and beautiful. She wore lovely clothes and dressed in the latest fashion. I do not ever recall her seriously scolding me. Often a look would be enough or the dreaded "Daphne Hylda!"

She encouraged me in many creative activities – from needlework and poetry writing to painting and play-acting. She took me to the theatre, particularly to productions of Gilbert and Sullivan, about which she was passionate. I was also bought a baby grand piano – but, sadly, this never became my forte! She was adept at shorthand and would take down the words of songs for me with admirable efficiency; I was vastly impressed.

She told me that she was the first woman in England to ride a motorbike and I can well believe it. She had designed a special skirt with buttons back and front, so when she was going for a ride she just buttoned up the two sections to turn the skirt into a pair of trousers. A truly decorous transformation.

My father

My father, Frank George Barton, was born within the sound of Bow Bells, in London, in 1869 – making him a genuine Cockney. As a young man, he ran a bicycle agency in Oxford with branches in Abingdon and Bicester. He was at one time, the Champion Cyclist of Oxford and was adept in riding a penny-farthing bicycle.

In 1911, he joined forces with another Oxford cycle dealer, a young man called Billy Morris, later Sir William Morris Bart., and later again, Lord Nuffield. Together they explored the possibility of manufacturing and selling a car that would be affordable by the man in the street and in 1913 the first Morris car was launched. At one time I had a great photograph of the two pioneers, with my father at the wheel of a large open car and Billy Morris alongside him. I was really startled to see a much enlarged copy of this same photograph, displayed in Longwall Street in Oxford, around 1960, and later, I understand it was displayed in The Oxford Museum.

My father moved his family down to Torquay in Devonshire, having been granted the franchise for Morris Cars for Devon and a major part of Cornwall. I was born in Torquay and two years later we moved to Plymouth.

Better than all other dads

My dad was better than all the other dads. He was very tall, had white hair, a white moustache, and was nearly always smoking a pipe. He often made me laugh AND he frequently used a monocle. After that, all other Dads faded into insignificance.

When I was little, I remember it was a very long way for me to look up at him and, when walking holding his hand, my arm had to go straight up and vertical to meet with his hand. I recall saying to him, "You can run the fastest in all the world, can't you Daddy?" His answer was too far up for me to hear but I was totally satisfied that this was the case.

Dad would walk me down to the tobacconist to get Players Navy Cut for his eternal pipe and mother's Passing Cloud cigarettes in their pretty pink box. Joy of joys, this was also a sweet shop. Dad would buy me barley sugar twists as he said they were good for me! Then I could choose. For a long while it was marshmallow, sold in strips about ten inches long and I would have one white and one pink. They were such fun to eat.

He taught me how to fill his pipe and not to stuff the tobacco down so hard that it would not "draw". It was an honour when he let me do it.

I was always asking my Dad lots of questions and he was very good about answering me. However, when it got a bit much, he had a standard reply to my question "what happened next?" - he would say "the balloon went up and the donkey came in to be shaved". This complex answer always had me beaten because, by the time I had digested it I had totally forgotten what I had asked him - so I went off to play.

When he wanted me to do something really well he would promise me as a prize "a putty medal with a gold hole in it" and I was astounded at the prospect of a REAL GOLD hole! I never noticed that I did not get one of these special prizes so I guess his generous praise was enough.

When I was about eight, Dad bought me a middle-sized bicycle; I stared at it and said "I can't balance on THAT!" Dad told me to sit on the saddle and put my feet on the pedals; right away he gave me a firm, straight push and I was off and never looked back. What freedom it gave me.

Kindergarten Finances I don't think I was spoiled for money as a child since I had to save up for things, but I do remember, when I was just tall enough to see over the bank counter, I watched my mother draw out twenty one pound notes all at once. I was shocked. She did have to pay a resident cook (£1 10s per week), a resident parlour maid (£1 per week) and a daily gardener (£2 per week) but it seemed like a fortune to me.

As for my own finances, I had two main concerns: firstly, it would take me ages to save up enough money for my dad's birthday present of an ounce of tobacco, and secondly, saving up three shillings and four pence to cover my halfpenny ice cream expenses for the whole two weeks we were on holiday in Newquay. There was always an ice cream cart on the beach, pulled along by a dear donkey and it was so good to see him again each summer.

All I had to decide was whether to have a wafer and work on licking it all around to seal it… or a cornet which one could lick right down to the bottom without getting sticky. Needless to say, I became expert at both.

Devices and desires
Dad liked to be ahead of the times and to indulge his interest in the newest technologies. He acquired one of the enormous, early wireless sets, which was topped by a large, tubular coil, which I guess served as its aerial. Strangely, an identical looking apparatus crowned mother's early refrigerator.

One day, when he was trying to find broadcasts from other countries, he shouted, "fetch mother", and to their amazement, we heard a male voice speaking in a foreign language, which mother immediately identified as French. Such excitement…Dad had penetrated the ether all the way across the Channel.

Another excitement was when our first telephone was installed. It was black and upright and the earpiece hooked onto the side. To use it one unhooked the earpiece, wound up a little handle and this would contact the telephone exchange with a friendly tinkle. Presently an operator would answer and one gave her the required number, which she would dial from the exchange and make the connection for you.

Nowadays it is commonplace to see people having mobile phone conversations in the street, and, in their own homes, via computer programmes such as Skype, they can not only hear each other but see a moving picture of the other person as they converse.

The first car that I remember was a Morris two-seater, with a dickey seat at the back, in what we would now call the boot. In the days of carriages this was a seat for servants. Dad would open it up and my brother, Ricky and I would hop in and enjoy being able to see everything around us as we travelled. If it rained Dad would stop and close the lid and we would wriggle through and pop our heads up behind our parents.

In those days, when we stopped to refuel, an attendant would serve us by pumping the petrol up by hand. Some of the roads were pretty steep, especially on Dartmoor, and sometimes our little car just could not make it to the top of a hill. Not to be thwarted, my Dad would drive back down to the bottom, turn the car around and go up in reverse, which never failed to work!

Barton Motor Company

In 1925, my parents set up a Morris Car distributorship, and appointed agents across Devon and part of Cornwall. The premises were on Ford Park Corner, Mutley Plain, Plymouth and comprised a showroom, offices, and repair shop. When they had established their agents across the two counties, car sales were booming, so they began to plan for a much larger, custom-designed building and obtained a site at Hyde Park Corner, still on Mutley Plain.

This substantial building was completed in one year. The splendid, marble-floored showroom was extensive, covering the full width of the building and containing a mezzanine section for administrative offices. The upper floors comprised a repair shop and spare parts store.

There was access to the rear entrance by a side road and cars were taken up to the repairs section in a lift that was large enough to hold lorries.

On the face of the building, an accumulating display, updated daily, showed how many cars we had sold that year. It is worth noting that Morris Cars were for sale at £100 before the war.

A few years later, the site next door was purchased and a petrol-filling station built to complete service to customers.

When the stylish, art deco building was finished, in 1930, Sir William Morris came to open it for business. During his stay, it was announced in the local paper he had declared my mother to be the finest businesswoman he knew.

To thank Sir William for performing the opening ceremony he was presented with a silver, authenticated, scale model of Sir Francis Drake's ship, The Golden Hind. At some point he kissed me and I went to school the next day a very proud nine year old, declaring I had been kissed by a baronet even though I didn't know what that meant!

During World War II, there were no new cars for sale, so my parents negotiated contracts to repair army vehicles, which, along with civilian car repairs and petrol sales, helped to keep the business going.

By this time I was driving and when the smaller army vans

were ready for delivery, I would get up at two am, walk to our building and drive one a hundred and sixty-six miles to the Army Vehicle Park outside Cirencester.

As there were no signposts or street lights, this was quite a feat. The reason for the early start was so I could catch a local train from Cirencester to Swindon and connect with a main line train back to Plymouth.

Our stout, concrete building survived the Blitz, even though a large bomb fell directly down the lift-shaft. It failed to explode and I wonder if some friendly worker in an arms factory on the Continent had left out the detonator. The bomb was quickly disarmed and removed so that repairs to the lift could begin immediately, as army vehicles were marooned on the upper floor.

It is only in writing this book that I have come to appreciate what my parents achieved. I was, at the time, not conscious of the link between their successful business and my comfortable lifestyle.

Chapter Two

School days

The very first day I went to kindergarten I was seated beside a little girl called Patsy and she looked after me. From that moment I felt I had an anchor in a very strange and unsafe place, with a headmistress I was still scared of when I was grown up! But Patsy was calm and knew the ropes and our friendship never faltered until the day she died some sixty-four years later. I used to get a bit jealous because every year her birthday came six months before mine, but no-one could stay jealous of Patsy for long, she was so easy to be with.

One Christmas, the headmistress told us we should bring gifts for the poor children and should only give things we really valued. So I dutifully donated the lovely doll's pram, which I'd longed for, and had only recently been given for my birthday in November. It looked rather empty but I couldn't face giving away my teddy bear as well, so I donated my brother's teddy! I felt really noble but my mother was furious about the pram.

I woke up one morning to find a heavy snowfall. Wearing my school raincoat, I took a tin tray and joined friends in Hartley Park Gardens, where there were several steep, grassy slopes. Snow was such a rarity in Plymouth that no -one owned toboggans. I didn't stop climbing up and sliding down until we'd worn out the snow and it was time to go home for tea. When I got back, my mother said, "turn around" and found I had completely worn away the seat of my coat. I don't remember her being cross – maybe because my face was shining with the magic of the occasion.

Later, at age eleven, both Patsy and I were accepted at St. Dunstan's Abbey, a school run very well by nuns. We went to the local church every Saints Day and about the same number of girls fainted each time, being overcome by the scent of incense.

One of my friends got in trouble because she was chewing gum in lessons. In a desperate effort to escape detection she tried to hide it in her hair. She came in the next day with a very short haircut! She was also the one who used to tease a modest and sensitive nun by asking her what was meant by "womb" and then enjoying watching Sister's face flush deep red.

For a while we lived in the country outside Plymouth; I asked my parents if I could ride my bike the twelve miles into Plymouth for the school sports day, as I wanted to enter the Slow Bicycle Race. They agreed and I won the race! Later I won the Flower Pot Race and these two wins were the pinnacle of my competitive, athletic achievements.

Patsy and I both made it successfully through School Certificate and I was awarded passes in nine subjects.

Devonshire Delights
Patsy and I loved this exciting city called Plymouth, where there was always so much going on. The vast bay, known

as Plymouth Sound, is famed as the second most beautiful natural harbour in the world - Rio de Janeiro taking first place. The famous Plymouth Hoe capped the promontory between the estuaries of the rivers Plym and Tamar, the latter marking the border between Devon and Cornwall.

On the Barbican, the celebrated steps lead down to the water, where the Pilgrim Fathers had set out on their perilous journey to America. Opposite the Barbican, was RAF Mountbatten where the large Sunderland flying boats were based and where ordinary airman T.E. Lawrence (Lawrence of Arabia) was stationed during the war.

The sturdy granite Citadel, which had stood ready to repel sea borne invaders since 1665, was next to the aquarium where, as a special treat one day, our cook took me to see the little sea horses swimming upright in their tank. I never forgot it.

Huge cruise liners would anchor and I recall the French liner, Normandie, seemed to measure the entire length of the breakwater. Naval vessels could be seen going to and fro the dockyards at Devonport and fishing boats set out from the Barbican.

We would go down to a little pebble beach, called Tinside, and swim in the Sound, run along the pier, or climb up Smeaton's Tower on the Hoe, which had been the original lighthouse on Eddystone Rock, fifteen miles out to sea and whose successor we could see on a clear day or by a winking light at night.

It was fascinating to imagine the life of isolation experienced by the keepers while guiding ships to safety.

I understand that today not one of the three hundred lighthouses around the British Isles is manned. Modern technology has replaced manpower.

Our great pride, of course, was the statue of Sir Francis Drake on the Hoe, where he had insisted on finishing his game of bowls, before routing the Spanish Armada. Many years later, my mother had a flat right by the Hoe gates. She joined the Hoe Bowling Club and to my surprise, sent me a copy of the National Geographic magazine, which contained an extensive article about Devon, and there, on the front cover photograph was Mum about to deliver a bowl on the sacred turf.

When I was visiting her one beautiful sunny day, we went with her bowling club to Torquay. On the way home someone asked the Captain if we could stop for some refreshment. She agreed and our coach drew up at a pub with a large, empty car park and a warning sign: NO COACHES. "Oh good, then it won't be crowded" she declared; so in we went and were all served!

When mother wanted clotted cream, I would run down to the dairy where there would always be a huge bowl of golden-crusted, Devonshire cream. I loved watching the woman scooping it out into a little container and I would bear this treasure home, where we would enjoy it with jam for tea or on strawberries or other fruit.

Every year we looked forward to the start of the strawberry season when we would go to Dartmeet, at the confluence of the East and West Dart rivers, and enjoy a superb cream tea of fresh strawberries, scones and clotted cream. One year I was climbing over the big boulders in the river when I slipped, dumped myself in the water and had to be taken home, ignominiously wrapped in a car rug.

Mother was a great one for picnics, even in the winter. She would get cook to make two Chivvy pasties, which she would wrap in a blanket to keep them warm. This was a Devonshire recipe, which today we would call Quiche Lorraine but with the addition of masses of chives making it even more delicious. Then we could enjoy a hot picnic in a beautiful landscape.

As soon as the car stopped I would run free across the purple moorland, alongside beech forested, stony-bedded rivers, pick wild flowers or just sit still on a log and look around me until I had absorbed the beauty of Devonshire in all its seasons and colours.

My favourite meal was lamb and mint sauce. In that part of the West Country there are many small country pubs called the Lamb Inn. I was convinced they all had lamb and mint sauce ready for us if only I could get Dad to stop and let us go in. To my constant disappointment he always drove right past. The only consolation was that when he did stop it was at an Hotel with a splendid dining room. There was so much to choose from, especially on the hors d'oeuvres trolley, that I forgot about lamb and set about choosing and consuming as many delights as I could.

Childhood travels

As a young child I found the adventure of Dad driving our car onto the Torpoint ferry very exciting. This ferry took us across the River Tamar from Devon into Cornwall. Dad would drive up the steep ramp and park very close to the next car. When the ferry was full there was a great clanking of huge chains and we were safely pulled across the river. In my imagination a Cornish giant was pulling the chains, hand over hand, until he had hauled us safely across the Tamar. On my first crossing I thought I was going to a foreign country and was quite surprised to find that Cornwall looked in many ways similar to Devon. The same beautiful moors, woods and sandy beaches.

This was almost as thrilling as the day we went on a train. As we were in the motor business I had never been on a train. One day I was invited to go with my brother to visit one of his friends at St. Germans in Cornwall. I was glued to the train window all the way and suddenly found I was crossing the Tamar again but by a different mode of transport. Boy, was I getting well travelled!

I was nine when I went on my first flight. My mother took me to the local Roborough airfield – and a field was indeed all it was. We lined up to take a flight in a small-cabined, single-engine aircraft. We took off, bumping our way over the uneven grass and suddenly I was separated from all the things I knew so well. Now the cars were tiny, as were the cattle, woods and rivers. I marvelled at how the pilot could move the aircraft in any direction he chose within the vast expanse of the sky. My heart was almost bursting with excitement. It really was shades of things to come, as much later, as a member of the RAF, I flew occasionally with my test pilot husband over the magnificent wilds of Scotland.

Much later in my life, when we travelled from Bristol to Wales for holidays, we liked to cross the Severn on the Aust Ferry. This valiant craft fought its way across the the strong tidal waters under its own engine-power and landed us close to Chepstow, thereby slicing many miles off our road journey. However, the ferry could carry only seventeen cars, so if the the queue in front of us, was longer than that, we would cut our losses and set off by road.

These ferries are now history, but what a joy to see both the Severn and the Tamar spanned by such elegant marvels of man's creation, speeding visitors to both Cornwall and Wales.

Cruise - on the high seas
When I was about ten, we boarded a Cunard cruise liner bound for Portugal, Southern Spain, Madeira, Las Palmas, Tenerife and Gibraltar.

I shared a cabin with my mum and on the first evening, when I was lying on my bunk and we were crossing the Bay of Biscay, I said, "Mum, I'm going to be sick". Typically, my mother said "Oh no you're not; put some clothes on, we are going for a walk!" And we did just that, round and round the decks until I got my sea legs and found it was rather fun flexing my knees to be in synch with the bucking ship.

One morning we were served a huge slice of vivid, red watermelon. I stared at it, feeling a little overwhelmed by the size of the portion on my plate. Seeing my hesitation, my mother said, "go on, eat it!" As food had always seemed to be my best friend, I set to with alacrity and was soon dripping with juice, and revelling in the marvellous sweetness, crunchiness and joy of a new experience.

In Las Palmas we saw children diving off the harbour walls for coins which the passengers threw into the dock. On shore, mother bought beautifully hand-embroidered tablecloths, which lasted seemingly forever. On Madeira, we went to the top of a high hill and came down seated in wood and wicker sleds, skimming over the specially built, shiny, cobbled way at a very fast pace, each sled having a highly skilled driver. I recall the first blue agapanthus I ever saw, growing wild beside the road. In Tenerife I was astonished to see pineapple plants, their fruit only two to three feet from the ground. My most vivid memory of the botanical gardens on Gibraltar was the sight of an enormous whale jawbone, which served as an archway.

Cap overboard
Mother planned a holiday in Wallingford, on the river Thames in Oxfordshire, so that we would be within easy reach of our many relatives in Oxford who might want to visit us. She then had the bright idea of hiring a motorboat for a couple of days and travelling down the Thames as far as Hampton Court.

We put our luggage in the boat and had only just pushed off from the bank when we saw a snake's head appear between the floorboards. My brother, Ricky stopped the boat on the opposite bank and tried to hit the snake with an oar. This proved unsuccessful, so we unloaded the boat, Ricky lifted the floorboards, got the oar under the snake and flipped it into the water.

After this rather dramatic start, we thoroughly enjoyed seeing many large houses with beautiful gardens, boathouses and their own moorings. It was an exciting experience taking the boat through the flights of locks and time after time we were astounded at the perfection of the pretty lock-keepers' cottages with their spectacularly colourful and well-tended gardens.

We had reached a stretch of river close to the Astor Estate at Cliveden, when we ran out of fuel. Father was sitting, rather nonchalantly, on the edge of the boat on the starboard side and he called Ricky to bring over the large can of petrol. This action upset the balance of the boat and father did what is now performed with great ease by underwater explorers … he went slowly head over heals backwards and disappeared beneath the tranquil surface of the Thames.

My mother and Ricky ran to the same side of the boat to rescue him, leaving me, aged twelve and barely six stone, hanging over the port side of the boat in a seemingly hopeless effort to keep it from capsizing.

Father could not swim but he always wore a Harris tweed sports jacket and fortunately, this held so much air that he quickly bobbed to the surface. As he appeared alongside, my mother and Ricky, with great relief, dragged him unceremoniously aboard. It was something of a miracle that the combined weights of a very large and now soaking wet man, plus mother, brother and a full petrol can were counterbalanced by my lightweight body. Meanwhile the cap Father had been wearing continued on its solitary way downstream. A gallant bather on the left bank dived in, determined to save whomsoever was underneath the travelling headgear. We were able to shout to him that the wearer was safely back on board, however the cap, joyful in its escape, continued its journey to the North Sea.

Dammed lucky
Another of my mother's bright holiday ideas was to drive from Plymouth to London, get the car craned onto a coastal cargo ship, which we would also board for the passage to Leith in Scotland, and so shorten the driving time.

It was fun being on a small ship and I learned that the wooden rims around the tables in the dining-room were surprisingly called fiddles. Their purpose was to prevent tableware and meals from sliding off into the diners' laps in rough weather.

Once we arrived in Leith, the car was craned onto dry land and we toured all around Scotland. I was missing my usual frequent holiday swimming and, as I was a bit of a waterbaby, I asked my father if he would stop the car and let me swim in the river. He agreed and I slipped on my bathing suit and beach shoes and plunged into the inviting looking water, while my parents sat in the car and lit up their smokes.

As soon as I hit the freezing water I was swept downstream in a very strong but unforeseen current. Once I had overcome the shock, I struck out for the shore, and using the current to my advantage, was able, with relief, to clamber back up on to the bank. I flung myself on the grass to recover and tried to work out what had caused me to be in this potentially dangerous predicament. The only thing I could guess was that just up river we would find a very large waterfall.

I made my way slowly back to the car where my parents were blissfully unaware of what had happened until I recounted my lucky escape. Still shaking, I got dressed and Dad drove on. To our astonishment, about half a mile further on was a huge hydro-electric plant and dam, which must have released thousands of gallons of water when I was in the river. Recently I found a warning on a hydro electric power website which read, "By the way, it is not a good idea to be playing in the water right below a dam when water is released!" How right they were.

The wild life of Dartmoor

When I was eleven we moved out of Plymouth to a house near the golf club at Yelverton, on the fringe of Dartmoor. I loved living out in the country and cycled for long hours on my own down into the valleys and across the moorland where the wild ponies lived, enjoying the views of the magnificent tors. However, it was a long journey to school and if I missed the connection with the school bus in Plymouth I had quite a long walk and could never win the promptness prize!

On my bike rides I saw so many wild flowers and welcomed each one in its season - snowdrops, lent lilies (wild daffodils), bluebells, broom, heather, gorse and wild thyme, scenting the air as one crushed it underfoot. I also loved to see and hear the larks as they suddenly broke cover from the heather and soared up into the sunshine, singing their tiny hearts out.

One day, I was tearing down a rather rough lane, going much too fast, when I hit a ridge and my bike flew off to the left and mounted the top of the hedge to await my pleasure, while I did a long, unfettered slide along the road, sustaining surprisingly little injury. I collected myself and my bike and decided that the excitement of speeding was well worth the fall, so remounted the curiously undamaged bike and went off to pick the wild flowers I had promised to get for my mother. This early zest for fast-paced travel would gain momentum in later years.

Dad was driving us home one evening and as we were passing several of the Dartmoor hills, known as tors, a big storm was brewing. First there was sheet lightning and then sudden, violent streaks of fork lightning, striking straight down and piercing the hearts of the tors, time and again. It was hugely impressive, almost as if Thor was at war with the other gods, but I was glad to get home.

Inside outside
When we lived at Yelverton we were about ten miles from the infamous Princetown Prison. One day the inmates made a concerted bid for freedom and a few made it to the outside. They locked the Governor in his office but were all recaptured since Dartmoor is not generous with natural cover, so the escape was doomed from the start. They were brought to court and my father was one of the jurors. The prisoners were all dressed neatly in suits and my father said that, in his opinion, the warders looked more villainous than the inmates.

Tyranny of the small ball
As we now lived a few doors from the Golf Club, my Dad paid a subscription for me and I was taught to play. It was

a very hard course, not made any easier by having occasionally to shoo wild ponies off the fairway without frightening them on to the carefully tended greens. Just ahead of the second tee there was a huge ravine, which had been a part of a mine. While most people's language became rather colourful, Dad told us with a wry smile that if the vicar's ball went down there he was heard to say restrainedly, "disastrous! disastrous!" but no naughty words.

I don't recall the fairway ever being green. The grass was a shiny, silvery gold and lay flat to its rock hard base. Playing a ball into the rough was well named. The rough was a few different varieties of heather all growing on strong wiry stems and worse if one got into gorse.

A viper in her bosom
In order to control the gorse, which had intruded on the Golf Course, at the end of the summer an army of men would arrive and set fire to it in a controlled manner, this practice is called swaling.

Of course many creatures would not find a means of escape and so one day I found a really long dead adder and thought I would take it home and play a trick on someone.

I wound it round my handlebars and, while no-one was about, took it through the French windows and wound it realistically in a circle on the carpet. I looped very fine thread around its head and holding the end of the cotton in my hand, ducked behind the settee and waited.

My mother was the first to turn up and slowly I started to

"unwind" the huge adder. She let out such a petrified shriek that I leaped from my place of concealment to let her know that the villain was already well beyond hurting her and that this was only a prank. I got away with a mild scolding.

The Teenage years

Back to the boys When I was fifteen, my parents thought I was being deprived of the company of my young friends, so we moved back into Plymouth and they bought a flat on the road where my best buddy, Patsy, lived. This was a really cool move, I was back amongst my friends, and could easily enjoy cinemas, the theatre, and swimming in Plymouth Sound. It also saved our parents a fortune in telephone bills and I had the joy of being able to walk easily to the school bus.

Having gained our School Certificates, Patsy and I went for secretarial training. As I loathed shorthand, I went to work in the Accounts Department of my parents' business.

By then the leading item of interest was boys, most of whom we'd known since kindergarten. We had grown out of girls' birthday parties, so now it was a matter of meeting for coffee in town at Boots (yes, Boots the Chemist was The Place to go!), swimming at lovely seaside places, hopefully with the right boys, and dancing in the new hotel, out at Yelverton, which I had seen being built. They had a lively band, which I can still see in my mind's eye, and remember the name of the bandleader - Francis Fuge. Gin and lime was *the* drink of the day or - if your partner was well-heeled – a Pimms No 1.

As my mother loved Gilbert and Sullivan, I was taken quite often to the Theatre Royal. As well as presenting musicals and light operetta, the Theatre also hosted variety, pantomimes and big band shows with bandleaders such as Jack Payne, Jack Hilton and Billy Cotton. Variety shows included singers, musicians, comedians, magicians, acrobats, and dancers and shows always opened with a line of chorus girls, dancing in perfect unison. Trips to the theatre were enhanced by waitresses bringing ice creams covered in Devonshire cream and served in glass dishes, during the interval.

The newly built Gaumont Cinema opened at that time, complete with organ and organist rising up from the orchestra pit. The whole place was decorated in the pastel colours of an ice cream parlour.

For me, learning to drive was a key item and at that time there was no power steering and we had to double declutch to change gear. Ricky taught me to drive on the moors – making me reverse, time and time again, around clumps of gorse without touching them. His tuition was so expert that I passed my driving test at the first attempt. We often gave lifts to those of our friends who didn't have cars, and I recall stuffing eleven young people into a two-door Morris 8, just for the fun of it.

We were all having a great time, when, on 3 September 1939, BANG! World War II crashed into our universe.

The King's Speech Following Neville Chamberlain's declaration of war in the morning, mother, dad and I gathered anxiously round the radio for the speech given by King George VI. As his words ended, we just sat there in stunned silence - unable to comprehend how events would unfold.   Seeing the film The King's Speech recently brought back the emotions of that moment - how time seemed to stand still as we contemplated the future with foreboding.

Most of our young men were called up immediately and sent overseas, including my brother and the young man I was expected, by both sets of parents, to marry. But fate was to intervene – and someone else would truly steal my heart.

1904 My mother, May Keeler and her youngest sister, Jean, the final two of ten children.

1916 My mother as a young woman

1922 Mother and Daphne, aged one, on the beach

1926 Ricky and Daphne on the beach near Bude in Cornwall

1927 Daphne age 6

Frontage of New Super Establishment

1930 The new Barton Motor Company building. Note how
the total number of cars sold that year was displayed in the
window below the company logo.

1930 Interior of the new Barton Motor Company showroom

1930 Opening of the new Barton Motor Company building by Sir William Morris. My white-haired father is standing just behind him.

1930 Scale model of The Golden Hind, presented to Sir William Morris when he opened the new building..

1931 Daphne age 9

1934 Mother and Daphne in the lounge at Yelverton

1936 Daphne age 15 ...

...ready for her first ball

My mother on the famous Plymouth Hoe bowling green

Chapter 3

The War Years

i. Plymouth's War

Graf Spee and the giant killers

Declaration of war was followed by a strangely quiet period, known as The Phoney War. An exception to this "quiet period" was the Battle of the River Plate, which took place in December 1939.

As some of the ships involved were from Plymouth, we were over the moon to hear they had crippled the German battleship, Graf Spee, to such an extent that it had to be scuttled, on the order of its captain, in the neutral water of the River Plate estuary on the coast of Argentina.

It was remarkable that the outcome of our first naval engagement should result in a splendid victory by the smaller British ships, dashing in and out of range of the German guns many times to overwhelm their battleship by sheer, raw courage and seamanship.

Word got around that our two destroyers, Achilles and Ajax, were almost home, after miraculously crossing both the South and North Atlantic, their decks awash from battle damage. It was true and I drove down to The Hoe to join an excited crowd, watching these two battered craft and their crews coming past the breakwater. How we cheered and how tears of pride and joy ran down our faces to see these gallant sailors safely home, as we waved and waved and thought of those who would never return. Francis Drake lived again in us that day – as his fleet of small ships had similarly defeated the might of the Spanish Armada.

Small craft were to play an important role during the War and in 1940 three hundred and thirty-eight thousand of our troops were evacuated from the beaches of Dunkirk, many in small, privately owned boats. Some rescued troops even landed in Plymouth.

Despite our jubilation at the safe return of these troops, Winston Churchill, our Prime Minister at the time, was deeply troubled by the perilousness of our position, particularly as all our European neighbours with accessible seafronts (i.e. Norway, Denmark, Belgium, Holland, and France) had already fallen to the Nazis. Indeed our situation was seen as so precarious that, according to the biography of the Queen Mother, King George VI and Churchill even discussed the possibility of suing for peace in the hope of staving off an unconditional surrender.

Fortunately this strategy was never adopted and, exhorting us to battle against desperate odds, Churchill broadcast a series of inspirational speeches which stirred our hearts and gave us the courage to carry on. Famously defiant at a time when our chances of winning the conflict seemed impossible, he declared to Hitler, "We shall never surrender".

The tide turns

Even prior to the major blitz of 1941, Plymouth, with its naval base, experienced a number of air raids. In September 1940, my parents took Patsy and me to Cornwall, to a tiny inlet called Port Gaverne, so we could get a few nights sleep. In glorious sunshine we journeyed through field upon field of harvested golden wheat.

We stayed in a house right down by the pebbled beach. Each day a home help would come, and on the second morning she just stood, speechless in the doorway. We asked her if she was feeling alright and finally she spoke, with tears in her eyes, saying, "oh, them boys, them boys, them beautiful boys."

Mystified, we asked her to explain and she told us "they shot down 179 German planes, I heard it on the radio - oh, them boys, them beautiful boys!"

We, with all our education, could not have found more fitting words to express the emotion of that moment.

This day marked the culmination of what became known as The Battle of Britain and was acknowledged, by both British and German leaders, as the turning point of the war, giving us our first glimmer of hope since the debacle of Dunkerque.

It is on record that Germany was planning to invade Britain under Operation Sealion. However without air superiority, Hitler knew this could not succeed. After our victory in the air, Hitler postponed Operation Sealion, concentrating instead on night-bombing London and other major cities. The Blitz had begun in earnest.

The Blitz

1941 marked the beginning of the heavy German air raids, known as the Plymouth Blitz. Being a prominent naval port, we received special attention and its geographic features made the city a sitting target for bombers on a clear night. On each side of Plymouth Hoe promontory were the estuaries of the rivers Plym and Tamar and the shining waters of Plymouth Sound in between, left no doubt as to the location of the naval port.

During a particularly heavy raid, German bombers blew up the oil storage tanks in the Barbican, which burned for four days. A friend of my father was a volunteer fireman who was killed when the tanks exploded. This fire could not easily be extinguished, so huge decoy bonfires were built on the cliff tops to the east of the city and set alight whenever enemy planes approached, in order to throw them off target.

An unheralded visit

A few days after the worst inferno of an air raid on Plymouth, we saw Patsy and her mother, both with grey faces, walking slowly up our road. They had just learned that their business, a four-storey department store, was "all gone, nothing left". We could not get our minds around this concept so mother and I drove down town to see for ourselves.

By now the streets had been cleared of rubble and as we approached the damaged Guildhall we could see, to our horror, that where there had once been a city centre, nothing was left standing. Shops, government and local offices, cinemas, markets, churches, commercial centres and sadly, some homes had been completely destroyed;

not one brick stood on another brick as far as the eye could see; just one lone, mangled girder remained, leaning at forty-five degrees; it seemed to be a metaphor for survival.

We got out of the car and joined a small group of people standing in a frozen tableau of disbelief. Then, to our astonishment, we saw the King and Queen, about ten yards away from us, by the now roofless, historic Guildhall and the shell of the City Church.

The King was in naval uniform but bare-headed, presumably out of respect for those who had died in the raid, and beside him the Queen stood, dressed in a powder blue suit with matching fur. They were completely alone – no equerries, military guards, police or city officials.

It was strange that none of us cheered but just stood there in stunned silence with OUR King and Queen who had come to comfort us. Their unheralded visit, acknowledging our City's distress, had such a deeply restorative effect on me that I was able to put aside the feeling of grief and replace it with the determination to do whatever I could to help. Later we learned that the place where we had all been standing was on top of an unexploded bomb. God saved the King indeed!

Presently, someone came over to us from the still-standing shell of the Guildhall to direct us to a church hall where we could give useful assistance. There we found Lady Astor, who was already working impossible miracles, by organising the collection of beds, chairs, blankets, water and food, for those who had lost everything, were in shock and feeling helpless. The immediate plan was to take over vacant spaces, such as schools and church halls, in which furniture and toilet facilities could hastily be installed. Our given task was to collect homeless people and bring them to a location where they could be cared for, washed, fed and rested.

It wasn't only humans who were made homeless; after one of these forays, I came home covered in red spots, so I went to the doctor next door to see if I had chicken pox. He smiled wryly, and informed me that I was not infectious but had provided a new home for a large number of fleas!

After the devastation of the city centre, the British Bulldog Spirit rose up and within no time, shops and stores were opening for business anywhere they could. One store-owner was first in line to offer to rent our showroom for the duration of the war and my parents agreed. Other store-owners found empty private houses or rented what premises they could, preferably near a busy road. Sometimes a large department store would have one department in one premises and others elsewhere.

Shelters – the luck of the draw
One evening, Patsy and I went out to play badminton at the local sports centre in a park. Presently the sirens sounded and we hurriedly gathered our belongings and ran across the park in complete darkness as, of course, there were no street lights. I found myself plodding through a flowered and there, at my feet, was a little old lady who had fallen in the soft ground. I just picked her up, tucked her under my free arm and carried her to the

air raid shelter.

Sitting on the cement seat that ran along the length of the shelter, I heard a tremendous crash and saw the walls near the entrance, move towards each other and then move back into their original positions. The next day I learned that a landmine had parachuted down and hit houses three roads from this shelter. These aerial bombs exploded on contact with anything solid and were capable of wiping out a whole row of houses.

In one of the raids, a member of our staff lost her brother, his wife and three children from a direct hit on a public air raid shelter. I had wondered how her family members could have been identified, until I recently heard an account on the radio, of a direct hit on a public air raid shelter in Plymouth, in which the dead victims were found, sitting upright, apparently intact, with dust in their hair, as it was solely the blast that had killed them.

Our staff member was tall and well-built and she immediately gave in her notice and joined the police. Courageous girl, we were very proud of her. Another friend lost her fiancé and a more fortunate one, who had been lying under her bed for safety, decided she could do better, so got up and went to shelter under the stairs. Soon after, a large part of the chimney stack crashed right through her recently sheltering bed.

Entertainment
As time went on, other young lads arrived in Plymouth, to man up the naval, army and air force bases. Somehow we still managed to enjoy ourselves, dancing out at the Moorland Links Hotel at Yelverton. If there was an air

raid in the city as we returned, no vehicles were allowed back in until the All Clear sounded, often hours later. So there was nothing for it but to join the line of cars and snuggle up to your partner for warmth!

Patsy and I went to the cinema one evening. There on the screen was a very American mother, saying to her daughter, "Take care of your body Maisie, it's the only one you've got". For some reason this sent us into gales of laughter, even though we teenage virgins did not totally understand the full import of the maternal warning. Later when we were both mums, with much increased understanding, we would go into fits of giggles recalling this momentous statement.

A similar, half-understood story, circulating at that time, was "What did Mae West buy a tin of Vaseline for?" and the answer was "sixpence"! The full significance of this also eluded us, but we laughed because we felt we ought to know why it was funny.

While we were in the cinema, the sirens went and we had to stay put for some time. When the All Clear sounded we went outside and found both sides of the street blazing and a tram on fire in the middle of the road – a picture of hell. Astonishingly, our car was undamaged and I drove over about four inches of broken glass from shop fronts. As soon as I could, I turned into the safer back streets. Both our homes were undamaged and our parents were relieved to welcome us back.

If there had been a particularly heavy raid and there was no running water, gas or electricity, mother would make up a good coal fire in the lounge, put on top of the coals a large biscuit tin on its side and place any food in it that could be cooked in this way, so we could have a hot meal or drink. It was astounding how soon the facilities were restored to us and a bowser would come round bringing water to the streets as needed.

No smoke without fire
We lived on the top of a hill in a top floor flat with a full view over the city to Plymouth Sound, so we could see the searchlights scanning the night sky for German aircraft, hear the typical THRUM THRUM of the enemy planes and see the bomb blasts from our front windows, which gave a panoramic view of the battlefield.

When it became too dangerous to watch events, in case of shattering glass, we retired to our Anderson shelter which was half-submerged in the garden. One night we saw smoke coming from our roof and realised an incendiary bomb was burning there. Dad got out the issued stirrup pump and filled a bucket with water while I got the steps and went to view the damage. I was waiting for Dad to pump up some water but, unfortunately, there were no lights on, Mum ran in to help and tripped over the bucket, emptying the water over the carpet, while I was waiting impatiently. Dad quickly refilled the bucket, I put out the fire, and we all made it back to the shelter. We were very fortunate because the later incendiary bombs had phosphorus in them and water would have spread the fire.

After the All Clear had sounded, we would usually go to the front gate to see if our neighbours were safe. Once we found one of the two elderly spinsters next door, wearing a colander on her head as a safety device!

Down the garden path

The only other time I was on the receiving end of Hitler's evil intentions was in 1944, when we were on leave in London, visiting my in-laws, and I was about seven months pregnant with our first daughter. In broad daylight, we suddenly heard the "phutt, phutt, phutt" of a VI German flying bomb, and as we looked up the sound stopped, so we had to race down the garden to the Anderson shelter.

Of course the entrance was not all that wide and despite mother-in-law pulling me in and my husband pushing me in I was still not making forward progress, due to the Bump. Finally, it was with great relief that Bump and I managed to wriggle through and let the two men into the comparative safety of the shelter as well. The VI exploded only three roads away.

Many years after the War, the centre of Plymouth was completely redesigned, as many of the historic buildings in the narrow streets had been destroyed. Unfortunately the new design did not take into account the tremendously strong, south westerly gales, which came whistling down the immensely wide, Royal Parade with nothing to obstruct them. As a consequence, it was not unusual to see little old ladies lifted off their feet and rolling down the street with their umbrellas blown inside out.

ii The Women's Auxiliary Air Force

1942 Joining up

The morning after a violent air raid, Patsy and I decided to join the RAF. Patsy was called up first, and was sent to the Intake Unit at RAF Innsworth, Gloucester. I followed a week later, and swallowed my first Armed Forces meal of the largest, slightly pink, fish flakes I have ever seen – at least three inches long and served with roughly boiled potatoes; I was hungry enough to eat it all. Then a quick check over to see if we were clean and healthy, and off to a hut where we were to sleep.

Patsy, having gone a few days ahead, had sent me a card to say I was to make sure I got a bed where my feet would be close to the stove. And I did, bless her. The ablution facilities were about seven minutes walk away, and the baths and basins never had plugs! The beds were metal-framed and three cushions, called biscuits, formed the mattress; two blankets were provided and as soon as you were dressed in the morning, these and the biscuits had to be neatly stacked at the head of the bed ready for inspection by the Sergeant. Beside each bed was a very small cupboard – the only storage space allotted to each of us.

The next day we collected our uniforms, and miraculously everything fitted. It was the weary Sergeant's duty to teach us to drill, beginning with getting us to distinguish our right foot from our left, and all to move off in the same direction at the same time without bumping into each other.

Next, it was off to Morecombe, where Patsy and I were delighted to be re-united for a while, though after that we did not meet again until war ended.

Around this time we "took the King's shilling", an actual shilling which indicated we were now members of the military and subject to its regulations.

We were billeted in holiday homes (complete with seaside landladies!), which were commandeered by the Services. We had lectures on hygiene and venereal disease and I wonder how many of us really understood then, what V.D. meant.

Over the drills and far away

While stationed at Morecombe we had to do more detailed drilling, taking it in turns to drill a large squad of WAAFs in order to graduate.

I shall never forget my first effort, with around a hundred girls on the sea front; I had them all moving in step and then had to shout "ABOUT TURN!" But I didn't have a strong enough voice and what I had blew away on the sea breezes. The result was chaos…. About forty girls came around, twenty in the middle ran to and fro not knowing which group to follow, while the other forty, blissfully unaware of the command, marched on towards Scotland. The twenty in the middle attracted all the stray dogs in the neighbourhood, who jumped about, barked and tripped up the unwary. The forty up front began to realise that they were running out of space and turned around to join the rest after negotiating the canine fun and games. It was a shambles! So I was posted to Blackpool to train as a driver (which I already was).

I did like to be beside the seaside

Although it was great fun to learn to drive a Dennis lorry, it was also testing, as one could not see to reverse except by having one foot on the clutch and the other on the running-board, so as to see beyond the canopy. We would drive with instructors up into the Pennines to practise, at first during daytime and later graduating to night driving; I was fortunate in already knowing how to drive, but for some of the girls, their first experience of driving was in one of these large lorries.

Blackpool was a great place to be, with the fun fair and Blackpool Tower, where we would go for the free Sunday night organ concerts for the troops. At one of these concerts I was surprised and delighted to meet up with my favourite cousin, Robin.

First Posting

Once I had completed my driving qualifications, both for lorries and cars, I was posted to Market Drayton in Shropshire; there was a large RAF station at Tern Hill, where we lived and a Group HQ where the drivers and mechanics were based. We slept twenty to a Nissen hut, the beds being laid alternately, head to toe, to lessen the spread of infections.

Driven to distraction

As drivers for Staff Officers, we were somewhat disconcerted to find that, for security reasons, we were not allowed to carry maps, in case they fell into the hands of spies. When we had to deliver a Staff Officer anywhere roughly in the "waistband of the UK", the only help we had was to study the three-foot map in the Motor Transport Office, memorise as much of the route as we could and then get going.

There were no signposts or railway station location signs and, if one got lost, no-one would tell you where you were. Police stations, if you could find them, were the only places to get help, but first they would check you out, together with any commissioned passengers. To prevent buildings and towns being identifiable from the air at night, windows were blacked out and there were no street lights. To make life even more difficult, vehicle headlights were shielded to prevent any beams being visible from above, and the slot, as I remember it, was about five inches wide by one inch deep.

In addition, governors were fitted to the engines, which prevented one driving faster than forty miles per hour; petrol was a precious commodity, needed for both land and airborne vehicles. Its importation was a perilous exercise for our merchant seamen, whose ships were a major target for enemy action, hence it was in very short supply. Forty mph was deemed to be the most efficient speed in terms of petrol consumption – hence the governor. However, it did make overtaking very tricky and hazardous at times.

I once made it to an east coast RAF station without getting lost, mainly due to my officer passenger knowing the route. Going west was another story. A trip to Pwhelli, North Wales, on which I had a spare driver so I could "show her the way" (!), was a bit of a disaster and we ended up in pitch darkness in a flock of sheep at the foot of Snowdon. Luckily the shepherd was with them, spoke English and directed us, in his lilting Welsh accent, to a local hotel, where the officer got us beds for the night, and we enjoyed an undeservedly luxurious evening.

A Wee Error
One of our drivers was taking an officer to a meeting and, after a while, he asked her to pull over by a wood as he wanted to take advantage of the cover to make himself comfortable. She stopped the car and he got out but did not quite close the back door. Presently she heard the door click, possibly from a breeze, and, assuming her passenger was aboard, drove off. After a while she thought it was rather quiet in the back and looked in the rear view mirror only to find, to her horror, that there was no-one there. Shamefaced, she had to drive back and find the stranded officer, who was, to say the least, not best pleased.

Not so much a coming out party, more a coming inn party
At last I was beginning to enjoy flying solo in life and when my twenty-first birthday arrived, instead of the middle class party that my parents would have arranged, I took my non-commissioned RAF buddies, male and female, down to the local pub to celebrate. What independence!

To top it off my Dad had performed a miracle for wartime and sent me a brand new bicycle. That gave me even more independence and much appreciated mobility.

Later, I was billeted with one of the officers and his wife and my only duty was to make a breakfast tray ready and take it in to them before I cycled off to the camp. It was so delightful to live in a house again, with a little bedroom to myself. It did not last very long but I loved it while I could enjoy the luxury.

Retreading my steps
While at Market Drayton we received a plan from the Air

Ministry to retread worn tyres, as rubber was imported and therefore in short supply. The plan included sending a staff member to train at Tyresoles in Birmingham, so a retreading unit could be set up back at the base. I was the one selected to go and the first thing I had to do on arrival in Birmingham was to find myself a billet, so I went to the Police Station where they gave me an address.

I was surprised to find a two-storey, circular, toll-house, with a fish and chip shop at ground level. The elderly lady who was running the shop took me upstairs into what turned out to be the only room, a circular bedroom with a double bed and a strong aroma of fish and chips! I asked her where I would sleep and she said in the bed with her! Wearily I trekked back to the Police Station and was sent to a new address where I was billeted with a really nice family for the week.

I did the course and got a hundred per cent pass for the written examination but there was no practical training. I was ordered back to Market Drayton only to discover the whole plan had been dropped.

My next stop was to go to London and appear before the RAF Officer Selection Board, which was a great surprise to me.

1942 Promotion
If I was surprised to be called to appear before the Officer Selection Board, I was even more surprised to be accepted. My posting was to Windermere, to the Officer Training School and I now wore a white hat-band to indicate I was an Officer Cadet. It was beautiful, though freezing cold, up there and the hotel, where we often met

for training courses, had gardens running down to Lake Windermere. The place seemed to be inhabited by hundreds of officers, so many salutes were the order of the day. On one occasion, I was giving a particularly smart salute, brought my arm up a little on the speedy side, upset my balance and fell over backwards on the ice-covered pavement. As everybody was senior to me at that moment, no-one bothered to help me up. At a later date, my husband taught me the RAF jargon for falling over backwards was "base over apex".

In due course, I was commissioned and sent to Grange-over-Sands in Cumbria, to train as an Equipment Officer. In peacetime this would have been a three-year, full-time course, but we had to complete it in six weeks.

I was granted leave and went home to Plymouth, where I had my officer's uniform, including a splendid greatcoat, made to measure by Gieves, an unbelievable luxury for which no clothing coupons were required. My parents were very delighted by my promotion.

1943 Taken for a ride
When I had collected my officer's uniform, I was ordered to report to Group HQ at Andover. I set off with my suitcase (no dreaded kitbag now) and the treasured bicycle.

On arrival I was shown into the office of a Group Captain Honey, and well-named he turned out to be. He informed me that I was being posted to Kinloss, in Northern Scotland and asked if I would like a lift in a Spitfire! WOW, would I indeed! I was open-mouthed with delight.

I thought this senior officer was a bit quiet so I stole a glance at him, found he was smiling and that my foot was indeed in my mouth. I should have remembered the Spitfire was a single-seater with barely room for the pilot, let alone a brand new, untried officer, suitcase and bicycle. What a clanger, I had dropped, hardly inspiring confidence that I could help to win the war as an officer! I don't suppose I was the first gullible girl he had teased, but at least I had been enthusiastic!

1943 An arresting story?

As no air lift was available to Kinloss for Assistant Section Officer Barton number 6451, I got on the train, dressed all posh in my new officer's uniform, accompanied by my suitcase and trusty bike. Endless hours later we stopped at the Scottish junction of Aviemore. We seemed to have been there quite a while when I saw two Red Caps (Military Police) on the platform, calling out a name. I remember thinking that it could not be mine as no-one knew I was there. How wrong I was!

Presently the Red Caps came down the corridor calling "ASO Barton!!" Completely mystified, I gave myself up! They took my suitcase and walked me up the platform in silence, with hundreds of pairs of eyes watching and noses pressed to the windows.

We were nearly at the Station Master's office, when I let out a stricken cry, "My bicycle!" So we walked all the way back to the Guard's van, collected my treasure and ran the gauntlet, yet again, of the banks of watching eyes.

Whatever had I done? Did they think I was a spy or an impostor? It was only then that one of the previously taciturn Military Policemen told me I needed to change trains. The one I was on was going to Inverness and I needed to go to Forres near RAF Kinloss. Phew!!

iii RAF Kinloss

Steep learning curve

The WAAF Officers' Mess was a typical, stone-built Scottish house with a pleasant garden and was only half a mile from RAF Kinloss. On my first night I was invited to the Base, to sit with the other officers where the Adjutant made me very welcome and told me I would be able to enjoy up-to-date films and occasional ENSA shows (Entertainments National Service Association). I was blissfully unaware, at that time, that my arrival had provoked a bit of nudge, nudge, wink, wink, among the younger male officers.

The main part of the Base was a Flying Training School. The section where I was posted was a Maintenance Unit. It was here that the Air Transport Auxiliary (ATA), both men and women civilian pilots, would deliver planes direct from the factories for testing, before they were sent into action. There were also planes requiring repairs or modifications, to bring them up to standard; these were tested by our test pilots before being transported by the ATA to front line aerodromes.

When I first arrived at Kinloss, I was fascinated by the large, half-moon shaped hangars, that were covered entirely by growing turf. It must have been extremely difficult for an enemy to spot them from the air.

I was fortunate to have a very understanding senior at Kinloss but one day he came into the office looking fed up. After a while, I asked him what was the matter. He glumly replied, "My wife is pregnant YET again. I only have to hang my trousers over the end of the bed!" This caused us both to chuckle.

He was very tolerant of my lack of knowledge and never let on to me just how limited my contribution was. However, in the long term, this fact was not missed by the Air Ministry, which was discovering that putting trainees through a three-year course in six weeks was like putting kindergarten children into the sixth form and expecting acceptable results.

There was a large blackboard in our office, listing the many planes needing attention and much daily communication took place between our Unit and the Air Ministry in London. To me these calls sounded like, "Is Wellington number 648273 now fitted with modification number BR73CS21?" To which my only reply could be, "Please hold, Sir, I will fetch Flight Sergeant right away".

Flight was a miracle worker and knew everything that was happening off the top of his head. I soon came to realise that the non-commissioned officers were the backbone of the whole military machine, so it was unfortunate that I managed, unwittingly, to embarrass him one day.

How to embarrass a flight sergeant
Flight, who seemed to know absolutely everything, while I felt I knew absolutely nothing, was also most understanding about the limitations of my training and we both knew it was unlikely I would ever satisfactorily replace my predecessor who had been sent to the front lines. However his tolerance was sorely strained one day as he took me through an aircraft, showing me that each

part was marked with a reference number, which matched that on the manifest in his hand, so that, in future, I could identify parts on the list.

For simplicity we started with an Anson – a six-seat, twin-engine aircraft - and I followed how he was matching the items with those listed; as we worked our way up inside the 'plane, I espied a small cup, fitted to a narrow pipe running along the interior of the fuselage and disappearing from view.

I searched for the reference number but could find none; so I called Flight and asked him what this object was and why it did not have a number. He did not answer but turned away, so I politely asked him again. He continued to study his brilliantly polished boots and said "Ma'am, I think you're being difficult." This remark stopped me in my tracks; if there is one thing I consider I am not, it is "difficult", so I took time to look hard at this anonymous small cup and pipe fitted in a highly technical machine.

The penny drops Why was the puzzling piece of equipment not numbered? Was it because it was unimportant? That didn't make sense. What was so embarrassing about this insignificant object? Then the penny dropped - this was a toilet facility for male crew caught short! It took a while for me to realise because it was totally useless for a girl. When Flight saw reason flooding my face, he was relieved that we could move on to the next object.

Meeting the love of my life

MacCupid at work

The first thing I noticed about Cliff was his delightful voice. The adjutant had said to me one day, "I think Farrow is your type." "Oh NO!" I'd said with some vehemence, "He's not tall enough!" My father and brother were both over six feet – so tall, dark and handsome was the recipe I was following.... however, I liked his voice.

I walked into the Officers' Mess one day and there was this same guy up a step-ladder, decorating the lights for a dance that was being attended that evening by the local public. Threading daffodils into a wire-netting cage, so that the finished product would be a golden ball, he was up and down the steps fetching the flowers, so I asked him if he would like me to pass them up to him and he readily agreed.

After we had this system going really well, I said, " May I call you Chris?" to which he replied, "you can if you like but it's not my name." That first encounter set us laughing, which was a good start.

Thrills and spills

There were many things I was to discover about Cliff after we first met. For instance, he had taken flying lessons before the war and, anticipating the onset of hostilities, had joined the RAF Volunteer Reserve, and was actually called up on the day war was declared. His first assignment was towing drogues to provide target practice for the ground artillery. I came to realise he was totally courageous; he had trained to test about one hundred different types of aircraft and had experienced five forced landings without injury, one caused by a pair of lady's knickers being stuffed into the oil feed. A strange form of sabotage.

In 1940, when France fell and some of our pilots were stranded, he had flown a Spitfire to Nantes, picked up a pilot, who had to sit on his lap and navigate, while Cliff flew the plane safely back to the UK.

I also learned he was delightfully funny, very kind, thoughtful and a wonderful dancer who had taught ballroom dancing as a hobby.

Cliff also knew how to waltz himself out of a tight corner, so one day, when he was about to fly a small single-engine plane, which needed ground crew to swing the propeller to start the engine, he had taxied to the correct part of the perimeter for take-off but, as he got there, the engine stopped. He did not fancy footing it all the way back to the hangar, so he set the engine correctly, got out, swung the prop himself and was horrified to see the little plane take off without him!! Luckily it stalled, came down nearby, hitting a muddy patch and pitched forward onto its prop, thereby putting itself out of action. He just let the scene speak for itself, "Hit a muddy patch on take off, sir", was his report to the C.O..

There were three test pilots at Kinloss Maintenance Unit and at this point I did not realise they were thinking up all kinds of mischief for me.

Fair, Fair Game
As soon as it was known that a female Equipment Officer had arrived and was a blonde to boot, I was fair game.

Requisition forms started arriving on my desk for such items as 2 gallons of striped paint, 6 boxes of straight hooks, 3 bags of dihedral*, and other nonsense. They stayed ignored on my desk.

*Dihedral is the angle at which the wings are set with reference to the fuselage; if the angle is wide the plane is said to have "bags of dihedral".

Score: Boys 0, Girl 1

Sorry, no leg shows today boys
There was a small airfield across the Cromarty Firth, at Dornoch, used as a parking area for aircraft awaiting attention. There was also a small equipment office, so Cliff asked me if I would like to fly there with him and inspect that office. I was both delighted and excited. He told me that the Commanding Officer of the Base insisted that I wear an observer-type parachute if I was to fly. Unbeknown to me, that type of parachute has harness straps, which are brought down from the back, between the legs and fastened with a clip on the chest.

When I presented myself next day, all three test pilots were standing in a row, chuckling like kids. I got out of my transport ready to get into theirs and go to the plane. Suddenly I noticed that all the smiles had been wiped off their faces and wondered what I had done. The boys, expecting me to be in my normal uniform of a fairly short, tight skirt, were looking forward to a good glimpse of leg and perhaps, a bit of thigh coming into view. What the boys did not know was that, this very morning, I had taken delivery of the first women's battledress – (tunic and trousers), and I was wearing it. Well, who'd be more likely to get the first one than the Equipment Officer?

Cliff later admitted that there had been no C.O.'s order that I wear a parachute.

New score: Boys 0, Girl 2

Was I bothered?

We set off in an Anson and Cliff took the plane literally down to sea level, crept up over a small fishing boat and down to the sea again, then up a small cliff over Cromarty, breezing the grasses flat. He repeated the performance over the water on the other side and then landed in the airfield - virtually two small fields with the party hedge cut away. I remember thinking it was a very strange way to fly a plane and I guess he was trying to get his own back for the battledress debacle and I was supposed to be really scared.... but I loved it!

New score: Boys 0, Girl 3

Fourth prank.... success!

As the first three pranks turned out to be damp squibs, the test pilots worked out something much more sophisticated.

We were making another flying visit across the water to Dornoch and Cliff was piloting. I had ridden out to the test flight hut and propped my bicycle up against its wall. We took off, flying directly over the hut and looking down, I saw, to my horror, the precious bicycle lying in pieces on the grass. I nudged Cliff and showed him the disaster; he shook his head and said "Tut, Tut", but I was truly livid. The bicycle was my only worldly possession at that time. I just could not wait to get back but, as we flew over the test flight hut on the return journey, to my astonishment I saw my bicycle was there, complete and resting against the hut just as I had left it!

Once we'd landed, I ran to my bike, eager to ride away from these tormentors.... the only trouble was, they had not tightened up the handlebars, so I jerked forward in both shock and rage and demanded that they put this right NOW. Straight-faced and apparently apologetic, they did so at once. Still enraged and frustrated in my efforts to get away... I sat on the saddle, but that too went down with a thump. It was unbelievable. "TIGHTEN THIS UP AT ONCE!" I yelled like a harridan. More apologies were given as I finally rode away, with shredded dignity!

Final score: Boys 1, Girl 3   (But I got my own back later on...I married him!)

Serious Reconnaissance
Having put me through a series of trials by ordeal, Cliff must have decided I was worth further flight-testing.

An unsteady first approach   In an attempt to get the relationship off the ground, Cliff rode his bike over to the WAAF Officers' Mess to invite me to go to the camp cinema with him. I was in my bedroom at the time, overlooking the driveway, which was bordered by a long laurel hedge.

Standing by the window, I watched this intrepid and highly trained airman ride down the drive and land squarely in the hedge; I thought to myself "This is a test pilot? He certainly isn't a navigator!".

On our next outing, we rode to a small town and found a little cafe where we enjoyed delicious Scottish kippers. These were quite a luxury during the war, so we sent a box to each of our families. Curiously, Cliff's nickname was Kipper Farrow!

We would also visit a very generous farming family, who lived within cycling distance, and who freely entertained RAF personnel with cream teas and other miracles; in return, our boys would go and shoot pigeons to prevent them damaging the crops.

Come dine with me
As the relationship was really beginning to take off, Cliff invited me to dinner with him at the Royal Marine Hotel at Nairn. Things were surely warming up and my resistance was low. We duly met and set out on our trusty steeds and presently I asked how far we had to cycle. He replied that it was about twelve miles. I was somewhat shaken by this but the coast road was level and we had plenty of time. I was so thrilled to be asked out by him on a proper date that I was not to be discouraged by the distance to the destination.

At one point, when we came to a small hill, being the perfect gentleman, he reached over to my handlebars to give me a tug up the slope. Unfortunately all that it did was to totally unbalance me and I fell in a heap on the road. No injuries were sustained, except to my dignity. It was only the second time I had ever fallen off a bike.

We arrived at this excellent hotel in good time, had a simple but splendid dinner with wine, increased our liking of each other and cycled back, dallying on the way 'to admire the view'.

When I came to write this book, sixty-six years later, I thought I would check out the actual distance and found that this journey was, in fact, only about six miles each way! Love is blind!

Standing room only
We had flown to Dornoch one day so that Cliff could fly a four-engine Halifax bomber back to Kinloss for repair. When he showed me this massive machine, I could not imagine how he would get its speed up sufficiently, either to clear the trees at the end of the field or even to get it airborne.

He looked perfectly calm as he handed me up into the main fuselage, which was empty except for a two-foot six-inch compass screwed to the floor. There was nowhere to sit and there was no door, only a five-foot square gap where a door should have been. He instructed me to be sure to hold onto the compass, which I did with total dedication, as it was preferable to being sucked out of the plane.

Cliff then disappeared into the cockpit and started the engines. When he had got them up to a roar that rattled our teeth, we rolled forward and he lifted the bomber over the treetops, banking to the right just yards above the sea and we were on our way back to base.

On reflection, I guess this was another test, which I must have passed with flying colours.

Love in a mist - more flying colours
One day I was flying with Cliff and suddenly we found ourselves in the midst of the Northern Lights - Aurora Borealis. It was so magical, just like flying through streamers of the very finest silk chiffon in all the soft

colours of the rainbow, changing and moving as we watched.

I felt I was just the luckiest girl in the world to be sitting beside my lovely man as we watched this magical display together.

No point in waiting

We both knew we wanted to spend the rest of our lives together, and in those uncertain times we didn't want to delay. So I went home to Plymouth on leave and Cliff followed a few days later to meet my parents and request my hand in marriage, as was done in those days.

Ordeal by inspection

I went to meet Cliff at the station and having never seen him out of uniform, was dismayed to spot him coming towards me wearing the most awful overcoat, of the largest, loudest herringbone tweed, I had ever seen. I was very tempted to put him straight back on the train. However, as his smile reached me all resistance fell in dusty particles onto the platform and we kissed; nevertheless, I made him take the coat off before I took him in to meet my parents.

Father said that if I loved him that was good enough for him. On the other hand mother was not impressed. She would have liked me to marry my former Plymouth boy-friend, whose parents were titled, and to make things worse, Clifford had a minus balance at the Bank. However mother could see she was on a losing wicket, as we were so clearly in love, so she sold my baby grand piano in answer to a Harrods's advertisement and this wiped out Cliff's overdraft, giving us an even start and improved relations with his bank manager.

Cliff's mother worked for a manufacturing jeweller and suggested we look for an unusual engagement ring design, which she would get made up at trade price. We gazed in Bond Street jewellers' windows enjoying the illusion of wealth. I found solitaires dull and too indicative of financial status, so instead I chose a distinctive square setting with twelve diamonds around a central stone; mother in law had it made and I still wear the ring today.

When our wedding date was fixed, Cliff sent a telex to one of his closest friends, a New Zealand, RAF pilot. On hearing his plans to marry, the friend cabled him, "Back out now Farrow, you clot!" But he didn't - my true love was true.

Preparations

To fix our wedding date, we had had to decide whether to marry in the safety of Kinloss or brave the Plymouth Blitz. We were very fond of the Chaplain at Kinloss, and he was keen to perform the ceremony but my mother had set her heart on a Plymouth wedding for her only daughter.

My childhood dreams of a white wedding were sunk without trace because it was considered inappropriate during wartime. Also one would not want to waste precious clothing coupons on a dress one was unlikely to wear again. So mother drove me to Torquay, to her favorite gown shop and we bought a lovely, soft turquoise dress, beautifully draped in a crepe material.

As a child, I was so obsessed with having a three-tier

wedding cake – my mother had to drag me past the window of any baker's shop where wedding cakes were displayed. During the war, there was no icing because sugar was severely rationed; however, a London firm made delicious cakes and supplied an attractive, and totally convincing, circular cardboard cover, beautifully piped in plaster with intricate designs.

Cliff's mother had my wedding ring made and engraved by the same man who engraved the Sword of Stalingrad, which was presented, by George VI to the people of that city, in recognition of their incredible courage in defeating the Nazis. I still wear this ring, though sixty-seven years later, the design has worn smooth.

I had always dreamed of having the joyous sound of bells at my wedding but during the war, church bells would have been rung only if an invasion was actually taking place. So there went my third wish. Nevertheless, I was so happy to be marrying Cliff that my childhood dreams counted for nought and we arranged for the wedding to take place three months later, on 18th September 1943.

Cliff's childhood friend, Richard, who was also an RAF pilot, stationed in Gibraltar. was to be his best man. Sadly, a week before the wedding, Cliff learned he was lost on the flight back to England, one of the many untimely casualties of this war. My cousin Steve, who was in the Navy and stationed at Plymouth, kindly stepped into the breach.

Wedding Bells (without the bells)
The journey from Kinloss to Plymouth for the wedding took me thirty-six hours. Cliff went to London to collect

his mother and they stayed on the eve of the wedding, at the Grand Hotel on Plymouth Hoe, where the reception was to be held the following day.

18th September 1943, there I was at eight am, in the proscribed five inches of bath water, when the siren sounded... on my wedding day! Happily the All Clear sounded soon afterwards and I was able to continue making myself look beautiful for Cliff. When I picked up the huge bouquet of red roses my mother had ordered, I swear it weighed about eight pounds, a test of bridal stamina indeed.

As Dad and I were about to get into the car, the skies opened in a torrential storm and we just had to wait until it eased off; I wondered if Cliff was getting nervous. Fifteen minutes later we were at the church and I was glad of Dad's arm, as I was so excited.

And there was Cliff, waiting patiently at the altar for me to join him. The ceremony, by our lovely vicar was over, the register signed and we were facing our families and friends; HE WAS MINE and I was over the moon. My friends told me that I positively galloped down the aisle! I always was a bit of a disappointment to my mother.

Cliff and I were the same height and I hoped he'd noticed that I wore flat silver sandals instead of high-heeled shoes, so I didn't appear taller than him in the photos. Same height is great for photographs – and also for kissing!

Off we went to the Grand Hotel for a wartime feast of Brown Windsor soup, chicken, for which mother had scoured the local farms, and apple crumble. The surprisingly delicious wedding cake was cut and distributed and the cover was to do good service at various friends' weddings.

On the way home after the reception, we stopped at Patsy's house and took the bridal bouquet to her invalid grandmother. I was very fond of her and knew she would enjoy the luxury of flowers in those cheerless days.

The honeymoon
Mum and Dad drove us to the station Cliff was still wearing his RAF uniform and I wore a beige tailored suit (not new) with contrasting hat and gloves, as was the fashion of the time. We got on the train and the guard, recognizing us as newly married, locked us in our compartment so, to our delight, we were alone. I guess guards did this a lot during the war.

We waved goodbye to Mum and Dad and then dissolved into private laughter. We had carried it off, we were man and wife and we just hugged each other to bits. I realise now, that without much consideration, I had tied myself for life to a loving, funny and courageous man. Well... I got that right!

Some time later, Cliff told me he had forgotten to book accommodation for the honeymoon. He had mustered his Kinloss pals and they called every suitable hotel in Devon, until they found a pleasant country house hotel in Crediton. I was oblivious of this hitch as I set out in the train with my new husband to Fuidge Manor.

The hotel was indeed delightful (the boys did well!) and my new husband made our honeymoon just exactly what any gal would hope for and I thanked him for the practice he had put in with all his previous girlfriends, making him so very expert at lovemaking.

We tried to behave like some ordinary service personnel on leave but on the Monday morning our wedding photo was on the front page of the Western Morning News so our cover was blown!

While on honeymoon, Cliff taught me to play squash. We also played on a slot machine in the bar and, one evening, won five pounds in shillings, shamelessly scrambling on the polished floor to gather up every coin. We spent most of it buying apricot brandy for ourselves and the other guests in the bar.

Then it was back to London to stay with Cliff's parents for a few days. When we arrived at their house in Enfield, his mother must have borrowed all the neighbours' rations, because every square inch of the dining table was covered in food she had baked or prepared in some way. There was no way I could do it justice, there was enough food for a battalion.

Soon we were on our way back to Kinloss and our new life together. It was many years later that Cliff said to me "Do you realise I never proposed?" Feeling indignant, I prepared to deny this, but on reflection realised, "darn it, he's quite right, I don't remember him ever proposing!" Nevertheless, we managed to live happily ever after.

A matter of extraction
When we returned from our honeymoon we stayed in a small commercial hotel in Forres. The only snag was an

elderly gentleman who sat at the next table and took out both sets of teeth, putting the grinning dentures next to his cutlery before he attacked his meal with enthusiasm and relish. After he'd finished eating, he would restore his teeth to their former location. I looked at Cliff, saw a soft green patina cover his face and knew we would have to move.

Our next home was in a small pub in Findhorn, on the north side of Findhorn Bay. It was quite close to the aerodrome but I would often have to really tuck down on my cycle behind Cliff if I was to make any headway against the strong winds. One morning we were astonished to see a Wellington bomber in the low water of Findhorn Bay, apparently undamaged. Reasons for its plight were not disclosed, but it certainly wasn't there for long.

A knock out romance
A few days after we returned from honeymoon, I was sitting on the edge of our bed, regretting that at 7 am and in freezing conditions I had to don my uniform and muster my troops for morning inspection, when I would much have preferred to snuggle up to my beloved. Test pilots are notorious for never getting involved in inspections.

Cliff was lying behind me with his head to my right and in a moment of mischief, suddenly dug both his forefingers into my ribs. Well... we had not really known each other long enough for him to realise how fantastically ticklish I am. In a swift reflex action, my right knee came up very sharply and caught him precisely on the point of the jaw... and knocked him clean out! I was left shaking him and calling "Speak to me darling, speak to me!" He didn't but I couldn't be late for the muster, so had to leave him out cold while I went to serve my country.

You take the high road and I'll take the low road
Sadly, after several joyous months living together, the Air Ministry, in its wisdom, not wanting to lose an officer to pregnancy, decided to post me elsewhere, as far away as possible. That elsewhere turned out to be my native Devonshire, about 500 miles from my beloved.

Unbelievably, after I took up my post I received a delightful letter from Group Captain Honey, telling me he had worked really hard for six weeks to get that posting cancelled - but to no avail. I still have that letter which you can see amongst the set of photographs that follow.

Many Happy Returns
13 years later, in 1956, we returned to Scotland for a family holiday, not too far from Kinloss; so one day we drove to the air base and asked the sentry at the gate if we might enter and look around as we had both been stationed there during the war. He made enquiries and we were allowed to drive round the base as long as we did not get out of the car.

We were very thrilled to be back and on our way out, asked if the same Chaplain who had wanted to conduct our wedding ceremony, was still stationed there. AND HE WAS. He had left the RAF for a few years but had re-enlisted and returned to Kinloss. We got his address in Findhorn, called on him and, to our immense, mutual surprise and pleasure, found him and his wife and children at home. He was thrilled to see us and our two girls and invited us to join his family for a great picnic and fishing trip the next day.

1915 Cliff, aged 3, with his mother, Elsie. Despite the sailor collar, Cliff was a budding test pilot, revving up for take off.

1940 My photograph of mum, dad, and brother Ricky, who is saying goodbye to us before being posted to North Africa. He returned safely at the end of the war.

1941 Daphne aged 20, shortly before joining up

1942 Daphne and fellow WAAF recruit, Lilian, during their basic training in Morecombe

1943 Equipment officer training course. Assistant Section Officer Barton top row, third from the left.

1942 Line up - Flight Lieutenant Clifford Farrow (back row, far right)

1943 Line up - Flight Lieutenant Cliff Farrow (middle row, far right),

Cliff (far right) with comrades on the ground and...

...in the air

Halifax Bomber - like the one Cliff managed to heave over the trees at Dornoch.

Cliff 1943

Meeting the prospective mother-in-law

June 22nd, 1943 Assistant Section Officer Daphne Barton ...

....became engaged to Flight Lieutenant Clifford Farrow

Mission accomplished!

September 18, 1943, wedding group - Cliff's mother and my father on the left, best man, cousin Steve in the middle, and my mother on the right.

FUIDGE MANOR, SPREYTON, CREDITON, DEVON.

1943 Postcard from Fuidge Manor where we spent our Honeymoon

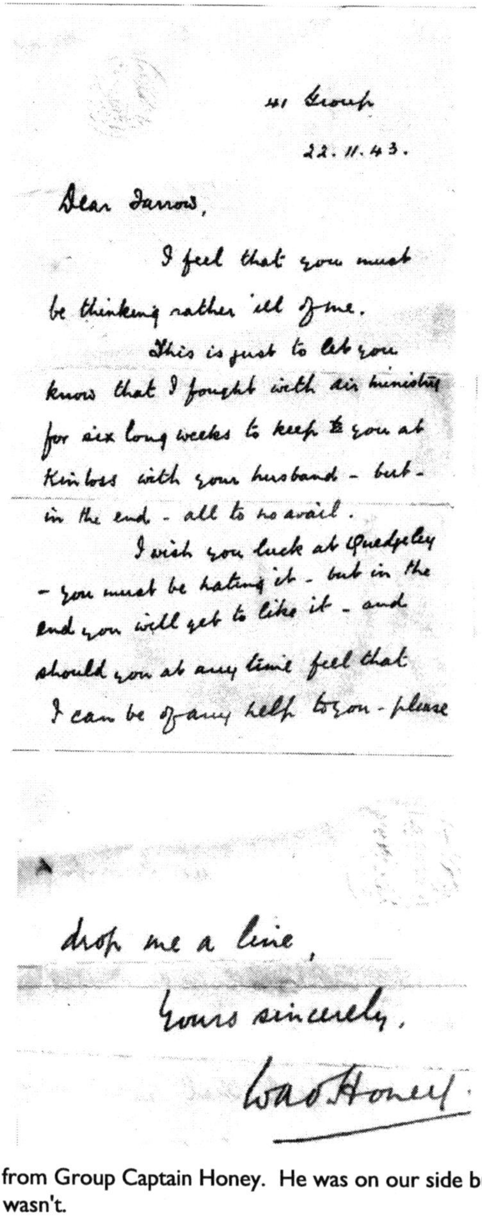

41 Group

22.11.43.

Dear Darrow,

I feel that you must
be thinking rather ill of me.

This is just to let you
know that I fought with air ministry
for six long weeks to keep to you at
Kinloss with your husband – but –
in the end – all to no avail.

I wish you luck at Quedgeley
– you must be hating it – but in the
end you will get to like it – and
should you at any time feel that
I can be of any help to you – please

drop me a line,

Yours sincerely,

WAoHoney.

1943 Letter from Group Captain Honey. He was on our side but the
Air Ministry wasn't.

Spitfires in their livery of black and white indentifying stripes as carried by Allied aircraft from D-day till the end of 1944.

Chapter 4

Married Life

1944 Back where I started

Ironically, fate seemed determined to thwart my plans; when I wanted to be stationed in Devonshire, to keep an eye on my parents, I was sent to Scotland and when I wanted to stay with my beloved husband in Scotland I was posted to Okehampton in Devon! There were two consolations; one was that my life was easier as, at last, I had a job in which I could be effective. The second was that I was within easy visiting distance of my parents – who to my relief, had moved to Shaugh Prior, near Yelverton, after a bomb had exploded in their road in Plymouth.

The unit was an Air Stores Park, hidden away in woodland, from which we stocked and supplied the RAF aerodromes of Devonshire and Cornwall. My main duties were to oversee the restocking of stores, to keep them constantly at six weeks supply; in addition I was responsible for ensuring orders for mechanical and other supplies from airfields in Devon and Cornwall were forwarded to our major supply depots. In due course we received these goods and passed them on to the airfields.

I also presided over disciplinary matters and was responsible for seeing that female staff were cared for appropriately. In one instance, a WAAF reported to me that she was pregnant; I asked if she knew who the father was and she replied "I think he was in uniform, m'am".

I shared accommodation with a petite, Australian WAAF officer called Maisie, who was jolly good company in this isolated outpost, five miles from Okehampton.

God rest ye merry, gentlemen, but please look where you're going....
It is traditional on Christmas Day for the officers to serve Christmas dinner to the troops and this we did on Christmas evening.

Maisie and I had done our duty in this respect, and as we came out of the mess hut into pitch darkness, four lusty airmen knocked me down onto the grass in a fit of uninhibited celebration. I was not hurt or even winded but I had lost my cap. Maisie dashed to the rescue and put it back on my head; as she said later, it was the only thing she felt she could do to re-establish my authority! Dignity restored, we walked away to the Officers' Mess to have our own celebration. Fortunately, as it was pitch dark no-one was identifiable – and I did not have to bring a charge for what was just an outburst of high spirits.

Despite the Air Ministry's attempt at enforced contraception, Cliff came from Kinloss to spend some leave with me and our first daughter was conceived, so, although I did not know it at the time, in due course I was to return to Kinloss as a civilian.

A story in black and white
While I was stationed at Okehampton, we received truly enormous quantities of black and white paint; this was a

bit of a mystery but we were assured it was correct and told that its arrival was not to be questioned or discussed. The vital importance of this seemingly mundane delivery was made clear on D-Day.

At this point I was not feeling well. It was known that I was pregnant and about to be discharged; meanwhile I was sent to an RAF convalescent hospital only four miles from Yelverton, where I had lived as a teenager. I did not have morning sickness, I just had an aversion to eating anything. This problem was solved by my swamping my food with Worcestershire Sauce, which condiment I have never been able to confront since!

Imagine my surprise and chagrin, when I awoke one morning to the roar of many aircraft overhead and learned that it was the longed-for D-Day. Instead of enjoying the news with my colleagues I was lying in bed. However, I was excited to hear that the vital black and white paint had been applied in stripes to the wings and fuselage of all Allied aircraft, so they could easily be distinguished from German planes and avoid being victims of friendly fire.

I had told this story over the years and one day, was watching *Saving Private Ryan* with some friends; right at the end of the film, where the Allied troops were in difficulty on the ground, Allied bombers, complete with the black and white identifying stripes, suddenly appeared overhead. My friends shouted out in unison, "Look — it's Daphne's planes" - and we all fell about laughing.

This wasn't the only ingenious device to come out of the war effort. We already knew of the bouncing bomb, used by the Dam Busters, and other brilliant ideas followed. The Bailey bridge, a pre-fabricated, portable, truss bridge was first used by the Military in North Africa, in 1942 and after D-Day, Pluto (Pipeline, Under The Ocean), carried a constant supply of fuel from the UK to France, beneath the Channel. The Mulberry Harbour – a vast portable harbour used to land transport and troops - was floated in sections, towed across the Channel, and reconstructed where needed on the French Coast.

Making a meal of it
In 1944, after I was demobbed and had moved back to Kinloss, Cliff was posted to Shawbury Aerodrome in Shropshire.

Our accommodation was in nearby Wem and consisted of just a bedroom and sitting-room, but at last we were able to play at being a married couple and I had to learn to cook.

After a while we found better accommodation in a substantial house; this was more suitable for a baby, as we had larger rooms and the use of a big garden. Cliff had a ten-mile bike ride to and from the aerodrome but he was a more competent cyclist by then! Sometimes he would bring home spare food from the NAAFI (the canteen at the base) to supplement our larder.

Food rationing had begun in 1940 and, because shortages continued after the war, was only finally phased out in 1954. We were provided with ration books containing coupons, that were cancelled or cut out by the shopkeeper.

Rations were pretty thin – our weekly allowance per person included four ounces of bacon or ham, two ounces of butter, four ounces of margarine, two ounces of cheese, one fresh egg (and one packet of dried egg every four weeks), three pints of milk, eight ounces of sugar, two ounces of tea and meat to the value of one shilling and tuppence (which converts to six pence in decimal coinage, but was worth a great deal more in those days). In addition, one could buy a one pound pot of jam every two months and twelve ounces of sweets every four weeks.

As there were no supermarkets one had to buy the different kinds of produce at separate shops and I recall there were endless queues, and much disappointment when items had run out before you reached the counter.

Vegetables were in plentiful supply and our landlady was very kind and helped me to get more domesticated than I had ever been. A large meal could be made from a variety of vegetables in a cheese sauce, using a full week's cheese ration! Living in a country town, we could sometimes get a rabbit or offal, without coupons, from our local butcher, aptly named Mr. Veal, and it certainly helped if you were obviously expecting or pushing a pram.

One evening, while I was still pregnant, we went for a walk into the country and found the most enormous mushroom, about ten inches across and an inch and a half thick. We bore this treasure home with great care and cooked it as if it were prime steak. Even for people with good appetites like ours, that and some vegetables made a plentiful meal and an enjoyable change.

Recent studies suggest the wartime diet, despite its apparent deprivations, was healthier than our diets today. This was partly because the wartime diet was low in red meat and dairy produce, and high in vegetables and cereals. Most foods would have been grown or produced locally and contain few or no chemical additives.

As well as food, clothes were also rationed but by far the most difficult to acquire were teats for the baby's bottle, as rubber was imported and therefore in very short supply and, of course, the war effort always had priority.

When Cliff was testing aircraft, he would sometimes loop the loop over our house; whilst I was proud of his flying skill, I wished he wouldn't do this as it looked so dangerous and he was so precious.

Victory in Europe was declared in May 1945. Cliff, who had been studying advertising and marketing via a three-year accredited correspondence course, was in London at the time, taking his final exams and I missed not being able to share the celebrations with him as I joined the cheering crowds in the main street.

A smutty story of oil on troubled waters
After VE day, we moved temporarily to a flat in a country location, where the kitchen and bathroom were one and the same room, and cooking was done with an oil stove. I was not too adept with this apparatus and, if Cliff was having his bath while I was cooking breakfast, the stove would sometimes suddenly flare up, sending oily black smuts into the air, which would land on his partially washed body and he'd have to start all over again.

Express delivery - no male on board

Annie did not arrive on the anticipated date of 3rd January, 1945 but made an unexpectedly swift arrival ten days later. My parents had arrived from Plymouth for the birth and were staying in our original digs.

One morning I awoke "feeling different". My mother was summoned and so was a girl taxi driver, the men having gone to war. As I stepped into the back of the taxi, my waters broke. A small tug of war ensued, between Mother, me, and the landlady. Should I be put back to bed or could we make it to the nursing home, booked in Shrewsbury twelve miles away?

The vote went to going for the nursing home. I was in the back of this small car with my mother and the landlady sat in front. There was snow on the ground making the road slippery, so the journey was frustratingly slow. After a while, I could hear myself groaning – I don't know why as I felt no pain. My mother was beside me and the landlady, in the front seat, was looking anxiously back at me; they were both saying "there, there" repeatedly.

Not knowing how much longer it would take to get to the nursing home, I felt I just had to stop the car. So I shouted to anyone who would listen - "STOP THE CAR. I AM SITTING ON THE BABY'S HEAD!" And indeed I was. My mother reached down and her first grandchild was born into her hands. In those days cars were unheated and all the baby clothes were in a suitcase in the boot, so she took off her scarf and wrapped it around the baby and put her in my lap. To our consternation, she did not cry.

We drove through the busy, Saturday morning streets of Shrewsbury and anyone looking into the car would have seen four very shaken women and a new-born baby.

When we got to the nursing home, the driver rushed to the door to fetch a nurse, who came out and threw up her hands in horror. She dived indoors to fetch the clamps and a blanket and ran to the car, cut the cord and rushed the baby inside to bathe her in warm olive oil. Another nurse brought an ancient wicker bath chair and took me into the home where, with great relief, we received the news that the baby had survived and was doing well.

Anne Christine Farrow, born 13 January, 1945 at six pounds fifteen ounces.

That was how I came to realise my ambition to be a mum. I really learned my lesson. My second daughter was born in a nursing home with a respectable ten minutes to spare!

My rather proper mother later scolded me for having my baby "by the roadside like a gypsy", but I think she still enjoyed telling all her friends in Plymouth about the drama.

After her unusual arrival, Annie (as she was later known) continued her life in great style. She worked as an advertising copywriter and, in 1969, became London Evening Standard Girl of the Year, appeared on TV, twice in *Call My Bluff*, and once on *The David Nixon Show*. Her wedding photograph appeared on the front page of the Sunday Express and, running a company that produced music for commercials, she was known as the Jingle Queen. Her activities were broadly reported in a long article in the Financial Times, together with a stunning picture of her in suede hot pants – displaying a length of elegant leg.

In her later years she became an artist and gained an Honours degree in Fine Art from London University of the Arts. She has four beautiful, grown-up daughters.

1945 Coming down to earth

After the war ended, Cliff was demobilised from the RAF and returned to civilian life. Of course the boys had a grand farewell party and Cliff suggested that I not wait up for him to come home. Just as well as he was not back in time for breakfast the next morning!

With hiccupping apologies, he told me he had woken up "the morning after", in a ditch. He had roused himself very gently, slid behind the wheel of the little car my parents had given us, and driven home.

It was a deeply felt farewell for him after six years of risky and exacting wartime service. He was awarded the Air Efficiency Award, for continuous outstanding performance as a test pilot. This was the only medal available to be granted to test pilots.

Going home. Where?

We packed all our worldly goods into our Morris 8, with the baby in her carrycot on top of the luggage. We drove to Enfield to Cliff's parents and the following day he went to Wembley to collect his de-mob clothes – belted raincoat, sports jacket, grey flannel trousers and a pair of shoes. Being fastidious about his dress, I don't believe he ever wore any of them.

Now suitably qualified, Cliff had been offered by Dick Brown, his pre-war boss at the printing and publishing company Arrowsmiths, the opportunity to start an advertising agency in Bristol, in partnership with Leonard Shepherd (also ex-RAF) who was an excellent artist.

Crashing into bed
So our next destination was Bristol, and, driving down from London we stopped for the night at a guest house in Keynsham, just outside the City. It was very cold and we were glad to have a meal and go to bed, which turned out to be a huge, brass double bed covered with a generous featherbed. A kind soul had put an earthenware hot water bottle in the top of the bed. It was bitterly cold and Cliff said the bottle should be down at our feet. He was very strong, grabbed the hot water bottle and flung it down to the bottom of the bed. We heard an almighty crash when one bottle collided with another one and they both broke.

The manageress was so kind and, totally unruffled, took the sodden featherbed and broken bottles away and remade the bed for us. I guess she had a warm spot in her heart for this little family with a baby, starting a new life after demobilisation.

Digging in
We found digs in Keynsham, sharing a house with the landlady. One day I was in bed with 'flu and Cliff brought home some cod fillets. The landlady came upstairs and asked, "How would you like me to cook your cod fiddelits?" Trying valiantly to correct herself, she repeated

"cod fiddelits, NO – COD FIDDELITS!" It took us some time to realise she was occasionally drunk. She got her quota of alcohol only once a month from her local off licence, as was quite usual at that time of rationing. So for part of the month she was relatively sober, having run out of supplies.

Shortly after our settling in, Clifford's new partner Shep (as we called him) and his wife, Connie, turned up, each with a child riding on the back of their bicycles. As, at that time, they had no car, they'd ridden seven miles out of Bristol to pay us this first call. I was hugely impressed, and took to them immediately, even though they were a surprising couple, Shep being well over six feet tall and Connie, his wife, just under five feet, so her nose only came up to the top button of his jacket. It was a relief to find the people with whom Cliff was associated in business were so friendly and easy to get along with.

Mr. Brown had loaned them £500 and let them know he expected them to make a profit in the first year. This they did astonishingly well, with a first year profit of £6,000, second year £9,000 and third year £16,000. To avoid using much of their capital, they constructed their own offices and furniture within a deserted school building in Denmark Street, (now occupied by Harveys of Bristol) and somehow managed to cope with the extreme post-war paper shortages.

Cliff and Shep enjoyed a fruitful partnership and an enduring friendship that lasted thirty-eight years until they both retired in 1983.

Locked in and locked out

As Cliff did all the travelling for the company, I could not borrow the car. After a while, Shep also acquired a car, a small two-seater Singer, which he kindly loaned to me for a few days, so I could visit my parents in Plymouth with fifteen month-old baby Anne.

When I was ready to leave, I put her in the passenger seat of the car, shut the door and went inside to get the suitcase. I had left the key in the ignition and when I came back, found the car door, for some reason, had locked. The baby was sitting there, good as gold, waiting for something to happen.

I dashed to the neighbour and he told me to use a metal coat hanger to pull the window down. This I did, hooking it on the top of the driver's window and pulling it down until I could reach the door handle inside. What a relief!

There were no child seats or seat belts in those days and Anne wasn't big enough even to see out of the window. Nevertheless, she sat contentedly in the front seat (a horrifying thought in today's safety-conscious world) for the whole hundred and twenty miles to Plymouth.

The journey was made more exciting because the ignition key kept falling out of its socket onto the floor as we rattled along, but, somehow, the engine kept running anyway. On arrival in Plymouth the first thing I had to do was to get on my knees to find the key before I could stop the engine and lock the car.

After only a few months, our landlady in Keynsham offered to sell us her house, retaining her as tenant.

Tempting though this was, we were very wary that her offer may have been made through an alcoholic haze and it might later be thought we'd taken advantage of her. Sadly, a short time after we moved, we heard she had died falling down the stairs.

Phew! A home of our own

In 1947 my parents bought us a house in Bristol, at the top of a steep hill called Briarwood, in the suburb of Westbury-on-Trym. Later we were able to take out a mortgage and repay them.

The first time I went to the house to take measurements, was on a very snowy day and we couldn't get the car up to the top of the hill. When I lifted Anne out on to the road the snow came up to her knees. We were unable to move in, at that point, as the only furniture that had arrived was a double mattress.

Furthermore we had purchased the house from a coal merchant and when I went to light a fire to keep the baby warm, found he had taken every lump of coal except for the tiniest pieces which I tried, unsuccessfully, to set alight. Amazingly, Anne sat there in the freezing cold without any complaint. Coal was rationed and even once we had registered, we had to wait a few days before it was delivered. So we took our measurements at top speed, grabbed the baby and left

In due course, some furniture we'd bought in Plymouth arrived and we were able to move in - thrilled to be established in our own home at last. I made our bedroom curtains out of hessian (one of the few unrationed fabrics) and decorated them with contrasting, Hungarian-style braid.

The house was already called Merrymeet and we were very happy there; we liked the name so much that we took it to our next house, sixteen years later.

Merrymeet had been built in the thirties and when we removed the wallpaper from the sitting-room chimney breast we found the original price of the house written on the wall. It was £825. The original builder had removed all the topsoil from the garden — something that would not be allowed today — and as I was a very keen gardener, I fought with solid clay all the time we lived there.

The house had many good points. It had two receptions rooms, four bedrooms, a downstairs loo, and a garage; it was one of only seven houses in the road, with open ground or allotments all the way round on which the children could play safely; it had lovely views back and front. The garden was well-established and boasted a double air raid shelter, which had been shared with our neighbour and proved a good playhouse for the children. I found it satisfying to grow vegetables, raspberries, gooseberries, red currants and apples for the family to enjoy.

Our hero in person
I was shopping in Bristol near the University one day, with baby Anne, who was about fifteen months old. I heard people cheering and watched as a large open car came slowly by and suddenly realised that our very own hero, Winston Churchill, who was Chancellor of the University, was riding in the back seat. I held the baby up in the air,

and tears were running down my face as I said, "Look, that's Winston Churchill who saved us all".

Another swift delivery
We often played bridge with our great friends Berry and Bob. Bob had been a Spitfire pilot during the War, protecting Malta – a real hot spot. As a representative of Bowater, Bob sold paper and Cliff bought paper for printing point of sale material, and from these mutual interests the friendship began.

One September evening, in 1948, when I was very pregnant with our second child, we were all playing bridge and, as usual there was a good deal of laughter and repartee.

After such a convivial evening I went to bed, my tummy still aching from laughter, which masked the onset of contractions. However, by midnight alarm bells began to ring and, mindful of Anne's swift arrival in the taxi, and Cliff's sensitivities, I did not think he would enjoy a re-run of that experience. So I called out to him, took two large bath towels as a precaution, and we set off on the three-mile journey to the nursing home, arriving intact.

I was taken to the delivery room and was plaiting my hair, when the nurse shouted at me, "Get up on the bed!" Just as well, as the baby arrived ten minutes later and the doctor was too late to assist at the birth. I guess I knew I could handle it by then, and the result was Lesley Jane Farrow, born 5th September, 1948 at a bonny seven pounds fifteen ounces.

The natural clown
Lesley was such a jolly baby and when she was in her

highchair at mealtimes, she would often have all three of us in fits of laughter. Even before she could talk, her timing was perfect, so just as we were catching our breath, she would do something extra to make us laugh, though nothing as obvious as putting a plate of porridge on her head.

When she was about three, we used to play Ludo as a family at the weekend. Because she couldn't yet count reliably, we all helped her, so she always won! Sometimes her counter would stick to her not-perfectly-clean finger and the counting had to start again; because her hand was still small, she couldn't cover the top of the cup with the dice in it. So, every now and again as she shook the cup, the dice would fly out and disappear; it would go "rattle, rattle, rattle, silence, silence" and then we knew we had to get down on our hands and knees to find the it. Once, after a really long search, we finally found it in the turn-up of Cliff's trousers.

With three A levels under her belt, Lesley joined a major computer company in London as a programmer and was quickly appointed one of the first eighteen year-old, female systems analysts in the UK. This formed the basis for her successful career. She has three lovely, grown up children.

The Brabazon
On Sunday, September 4th 1949, while we were still living in Briarwood, I was upstairs when I heard a tremendous roaring noise that shook the whole house.

Running to the front bedroom I saw an unbelievably huge aircraft labouring to clear our hill. I thought it was going to come in the front door but it banked away gradually and thundered on its way. It was the first test flight of the Brabazon, the wonder plane of the time, built by the Bristol Aircraft Company.

I had become so used to the perpetual noise from the engine test beds at Filton, that I was taken aback by the proximity of the aircraft, its overwhelming size, and the deafening noise when it was close.

To give some idea of how enormous this plane appeared to us then, the largest aircraft we'd ever seen was the huge Lancaster Bomber which had a wingspan of thirty-one meters, fuselage length of twenty-one metres and height of six metres. The Brabazon's wingspan measured seventy metres (ten point five metres wider than a jumbo jet); the fuselage was fifty-four metres and the height fifteen metres. She is still the largest aircraft ever built in the UK and had a greater wingspan than any modern airliner.

It's requirement was to provide luxurious travel from London to New York for a hundred or so passengers – and this specification turned out to be it's downfall as the market for it would prove to be too small.

Nevertheless, its design pioneered many technical advancements that are standard in today's airliners, such as cabin pressurization, which allowed the craft to fly at higher altitudes thus saving on fuel and consequently weight. It was also the first aircraft to incorporate fully powered flying controls and air conditioning.

Many years later, our new offices, on the twelfth floor of

Tower House in the centre of Bristol, gave us a marvellous vantage point for viewing the test flights of the beautiful Concorde, whose passenger capacity was also one hundred. This airliner was also built by BAC, in association with the French aerospace company, Aerospatiale and demonstrated the immense progress of aeronautical design since Cliff's days as a test pilot.

Domestic developments - glorious freedoms

I well remember the first time I bought Daz detergent, it was so exciting, so efficient, so NOT SOAP. At that time, I belonged to the Bristol Mothercraft Club and was so keen to share my discovery, I even gave a talk and demonstration on the subject at one of our regular meetings.

I used to make the childrens' party frocks. Imagine my unreserved glee when I first spotted a washable pink nylon fabric, flock-printed with white lily of the valley sprigs. I could hardly wait to get home and start making it up for Annie. Fancy the freedom of being able to WASH a party frock! Annie was the elder child and Lesley was so good-natured she would say to me "Am I big enough yet to wear the pink party frock?"

At my kind-hearted mother-in-law's insistence, Cliff bought us a washing machine with an integral electric wringer, unfortunately, long after the nappy years were over. Prior to its arrival, we had scrubbed washing on a washboard and wrung it out through a small, hand-operated mangle, which was attached to the porcelain sink when needed.

We still had no drier, so when it was raining we hung the

washing on an airing rack above the stove. This small anthracite stove in the corner of the kitchen, heated the water during the winter and kept the kitchen cosy. The ashes had to be emptied every day, causing smuts to fly around the kitchen, so we had to make sure we'd taken down the washing before doing this. But jacket potatoes, slow cooked in the cinder tray, had a delicious smoky taste.

Our next luxury was a refrigerator, as our larder was sited, inexplicably, on the south-facing wall of the kitchen and in a hot summer I could almost cook in it. Things put in overnight were frequently off the next morning. Although the refrigerator had a small freezer compartment in which you could freeze and store ice cream, we did not own a freezer until we moved house sixteen years later.

Gradually, more labour-saving electrical gadgets for the kitchen were acquired, including whisks, mixers, toasters, and kettles. The final luxury we afforded, a while after we moved house in the 1960's, was gas central heating.

Chapter 5

Florriedays

A rose by any other name

As I was not too strong in my twenties, Cliff looked for a home help for me. He asked the advice of his office cleaner and she jumped at the opportunity to help with the housework and the two girls, aged four and twelve months. Her name was Mrs Margaret Bidder, she came to us in 1949, at the age of sixty-five and retired from both jobs at eighty. During all those years, she would get the early bus to the offices and then come on to me, often with information about Cliff's appointments for the week – "I see the Boss is going to Manchester on Thursday", she'd say, having read his diary! This was often news to me.

What a treasure she turned out to be. She was large and strong and tackled anything with vigour; washing, ironing, and spring cleaning and she adored baby-sitting, sometimes staying overnight by choice and going directly to clean the offices the next day. She was also a great cook.

This is how she eventually came by the name of Florrie. The girls would sometimes go and stay with my mother in Plymouth, and Mother had a home help called Florrie, so Lesley decided that all home helps were called Florrie and when she came home, she called Mrs Bidder "Florrie". When I asked her what Mrs Bidder's full name would be, she said, without hesitation, "Florrie Farrow", as though I was stupid not to know this; it so amused us that the name stuck and Mrs Bidder was happy to be called Florrie from that day on.

A friend in high places
When Florrie went to our first floor offices in Bristol, at about six am, she would work away while listening for the chink of bottles, which announced that the milkman was close at hand. She would then go downstairs and get a bottle of milk for her breakfast.

She was in the process of doing this one morning, when the main front door slammed behind her and her key was still upstairs. She found the milkman and, in a state of panic, pleaded for his help.

"Don't you worry, missus" he said and asked her to point out which windows belonged to our suite of offices. In seconds he had shimmied up the outside wall, opened a window, let himself in, run down the stairs and was back beside her in the street. Holding the door open for her, he said "Here's your milk, missus". Florrie was astounded and asked him how he did it. "I'm a cat burglar" he replied and was gone on his rounds. We never knew whether he was teasing her or not.

An unexpected silence
A whoopee cushion is a small rubber cushion filled with air. If anyone sits on it there will be a noisy and embarrassing burst of wind...and that is the joke.

Our two girls bought one to tease Florrie, and put it

under the seat cushion in an armchair in the sitting-room. They then had to persuade her to sit in the sitting room, as she had the servant's attitude that this was not an OK thing to do. After much persuasion, Florrie finally sat in the big chair to please the girls.

Well...Florrie was a lady of ample proportions and there was total silence, as the whoopee cushion was completely smothered and never stood a chance to perform. This very silence reduced the girls to hysterics when they realised what had happened.

Alerted by the noise, I came into the room to find both children rolling about on the carpet, clutching their midriffs. Neither Florrie nor I had the slightest idea why and we had to wait until the girls regained some control of themselves. Once they had explained how Florrie had inadvertently foiled their game, we all joined in the laughter.

Mrs Malaprop
Florrie had some wonderful sayings, which we learned to accept with carefully straightened faces. Because they were too precious to lose, I kept a little notepad and pencil nearby when she was there, so I could write them down before I forgot them. This I had to hide, in case she found it. Here are a few treasures from her unique slant on the English language.

In philosophic mood one day, she announced, "There are times when we have to saddle our own canoe". I agreed.

Proudly showing me a photo of her elder granddaughter, she indicated, "and here she is, sitting on a bench in the park, all decomposed like"; and regarding her other granddaughter, who had put on some weight, she told me dismissively "it's only puffy fat".

Flourishing her daily paper one morning, she divulged the astonishing information that "in Australia they have push babies, wallababies and burgies."

On another occasion, she said with concern "Oh madam, you have been out in the garden all this time working like a truncheon!"

We put some water snails in the goldfish bowl to help to keep the water clean. The snails laid a large number of eggs and Florrie was admiring their feat saying, "just look at all that precreation!"

Acknowledging the good behaviour of my girls, in never feigning illness, she declared, " I've never known either of your girls to swing the leg".

Telling me about a wedding present she had bought for one of the secretaries in our office, she announced, "I bought her a Priorex carresole". "Very good of you", I replied. And on the subject of presents, I was battling with wrapping an awkward parcel till she helpfully suggested that I "stick it down with Secotape".

When our next door neighbour's wife died, he asked me if I would stay in the house with her body, as he had to go into town to handle urgent matters. I did this willingly and a few days later he asked me out to lunch to thank me for doing this small favour. When Florrie heard that I had accepted this invitation, she bristled in stout defence of her boss (Cliff) and said in serious tones "I do hope you are not going in for one of them candlestine affairs!"

Florrie "on holiday"

My parents booked a self-catering holiday for all of us in a flat over the Post Office in the Cornish village of Polzeath – just ten yards from the beach. Mum and Dad enjoyed spending time with their first grandchildren and, in those days, Polzeath was just about perfect for family holidays.

We explained this to Florrie and asked if she would like to come with us and cook for the family. She was so excited and said "Oh Ma'am, I've never been on holiday before". My heart ached for her. She came for many holidays with us after that and was never fussed about how many people she cooked for, it was just so exciting for her to see new places.

The girls would ask Florrie what she was going to pack for her holiday and her stock answers were either "a string of beads and me garters" or " my knickers with the flowers on the knee". Her knees had to be seen to be believed. They were flat, dimpled and about ten inches across; her knickers were actually bloomers and really did have flowers on the knee.

In those days, bed-linen was not provided for self-catering holidays and as we did not have room for it in the car, we always forwarded it by rail, and the railway company would deliver it to the holiday venue. Amazingly, this service was always reliable.

At Polzeath, the fish and chip van would come once a week and, as soon as the tantalizing aroma reached our noses, we knew we could let Florrie have some time off from the cooker. Otherwise, we could buy everything we needed from the Post Office shop.

One day Florrie walked down the beach with Lesley, who was about three, to watch Annie surfing. A big wave knocked over a small boy and Florrie asked Annie why she had not helped him. Annie's reply was. "My mummy told me never to speak to strange men".

Driving to Cornwall from Bristol, with five aboard our tiny car, was quite a feat; for Florrie, eating in a restaurant was unbelievably good fortune. On her first trip with us, she fell asleep after lunch in the back of the car and, on waking, pulled herself upright by the door handle; the door flew open, almost dragging her out, but she saved herself and slammed it shut.

None of us realised that the book Annie had been reading had fallen out of the car during this episode. As children do, she had written her full name and address in the front, including The World, and The Universe. Some really caring person had picked up the book by the roadside and posted it back to us. Annie was thrilled to receive it and wrote and thanked them.

Later, we went on holiday to Bournemouth and Florrie came with us again, to do the cooking. The kitchen was no larger than a big cupboard, so when she leaned over, her bottom shut the oven door. Our north country landlady would often come down from her flat to visit us; she was very tiny and would gaze up into my face and say in her Lancashire accent, "Ee luv, are they your own teeth?" I assured her that they were and she was suitably impressed. At eighty-nine, they are still my own.

At Treyarnon, in Cornwall, I did the shopping and Florrie cooked for eleven of us - we four, plus my parents, Florrie and another family of four. We did not know at the time we booked, that there was no mains water, so our two young dads had to get busy every morning pumping up enough water to fill the large tank before they were allowed out to play golf. We were only yards from the beautiful beach and the other wife and I took turns at helping Florrie.

On a later holiday in the Cornish cove of Crackington Haven, Cliff caught a five pound sea bream and carried it triumphantly up the forty-two steps to the house and into the kitchen; Florrie gave it her immediate attention, baked it whole in the oven and we all enjoyed a superb supper.

Happily for Florrie, her son, Jim, who lived not far from Crackington Haven, was able to come and take her out for a day's treat while we were there.

Jim's Teeth
Florrie's splendid son had been a career sergeant major in the army and she told me the following tale, which had been given front page prominence in an English newspaper and was headed "Sergeant Major loses his bite".

Jim was stationed in Gibraltar and was assembling his troops beside one of the docks. He opened his mouth to give a penetrating command and both sets of dentures flew out into the dock. A search party made determined efforts to recover them, but to no avail.

In 2008 I read an article about a naval officer on board a ship in Gibraltar dock during WWII. He'd flung his arm out to indicate something and his gold watch had slipped off his wrist and into the water. Concerted efforts failed to find it. Recently, when some work was being done on this same dock, his gold watch was found. Persistent tracking of records of the earlier event actually located the owner, the watch was restored to him and…. it was still in working order! Did they ever find Jim's teeth, I wonder?

Our treasure stayed until she was eighty years old and was still cleaning our offices until the day that she fell down the stairs. She was not badly hurt but as she was in the premises alone from six am, five days a week, it seemed prudent for her to retire and we gave her a farewell party at the office and an engraved silver tray. She went to live the rest of her days happily with her beloved son.

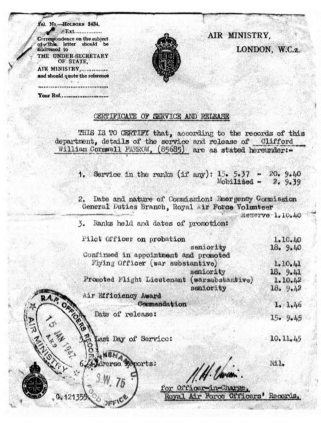

AIR MINISTRY,

LONDON, W.C.2.

CERTIFICATE OF SERVICE AND RELEASE

THIS IS TO CERTIFY that, according to the records of this
department, details of the service and release of   Clifford
William Cornwall FARROW, (85685)   are as stated hereunder:-

1. Service in the ranks (if any): 15. 5.37 - 20. 9.40
                                   Mobilised -   2. 9.39

2. Date and nature of Commission: Emergency Commission
General Duties Branch, Royal Air Force Volunteer
                                       Reserve 1.10.40

3. Ranks held and dates of promotion:

Pilot Officer on probation   1.10.40
                              seniority   18. 9.40
Confirmed in appointment and promoted
  Flying Officer (war substantive)   1.10.41
                              seniority   18. 9.41
Promoted Flight Lieutenant (war substantive)   1.10.42
                              seniority   18. 9.42
Air Efficiency Award
               Commendation   1. 1.46

Date of release: 15. 9.45

5. Last Day of Service: 10.11.45

6. Adverse Reports: Nil.

                                for Officer-in-Charge,
                        Royal Air Force Officers' Records.

G. 121355

Cliff's RAF release papers

1946 Anne aged one, on the bonnet of the car she was shortly to be locked in. Her coat was made from one of my mother's old dresses to save clothing coupons.

1947 Cliff and Anne in Keynsham

1950 My parents at the twenty-fifth anniversary of the Barton Motor Company. Note the vintage car beside the 'modern' Morris Minor and the ever-present Passing Cloud cigarette in my mum's hand.

1950 My father driving us in an open vintage car. The girls look miserable because it was freezing cold!

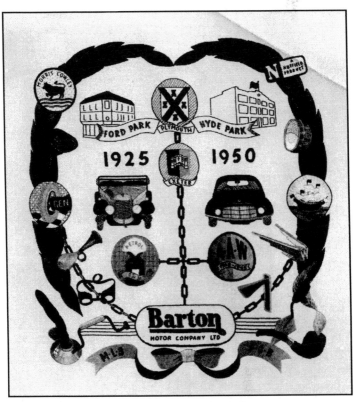

1950 the sampler I embroidered for the twenty-fifth anniversary of the Barton Motor Company. It depicts my father's pipe dream and my mother's clerical and business abilities. The left hand side represents the early aspects of motoring and the right hand side the modern aspects, like the new indicator, so you didn't have to stick your arm out of the window to show which way you were turning! AAW denotes the company's appointment as an Army Auxiliary Workshop during the war.

My mother, May Lilian Barton, age 53

My father, Frank George Barton, age 86

1951 Anne and Lesley in the garden at Briarwood

1952 The Farrow family in the garden at Merrymeet

1952 Our treasure, Florrie, with the two girls at Polzeath

1969 Florrie at Annie's wedding, about to wipe a tear from her eye.

Chapter 6

The tribulations of travel

W C field *

In the days when there were no motorways, the journey from Bristol down to Cornwall would take about six hours and there were no handy roadside conveniences. On one trip, Cliff stopped by a field gate in Devon so the girls and I could go in and make ourselves comfortable.

Once in a quiet corner, I attended to the girls and thought it prudent for me also to spend a penny. I was just pulling up my trousers, when a voice right behind me said in a rich, familiar Devonshire accent "Mind you close the gate behind you m'dear". I have excellent hearing but had heard not a sound of the farmer's approach. I assured him that I would do exactly as he asked and I think I blushed from my top right down to my bottom. I wondered afterwards if this was his regular peepshow entertainment during summer holidays. His stealthy approach was worthy of James Bond!

for those who've not heard of him, W.C. Fields was an American actor and comedian.

In charge of the Guard

When they were quite young, the children would go on the train to my mother, for a holiday in Plymouth. This began when Annie was eight years old and Lesley only five. Today one would not dream of putting such young children on a train without an adult, but then it was quite normal.

I always pinned a notice on their coats, which read, "in charge of the Guard", whom we had tipped to look after them and to see that they got off safely at Plymouth. Recently my daughter told me that they thought this meant *they* were in charge of the Guard – but had no idea how they were were supposed to look after him!

Being familiar with their substantial appetites, I would prepare plenty of pork and pickle sandwiches, biscuits and fruit. I put them on the train at Bristol, Temple Meads at about nine am, for the three to four hour journey to Plymouth, imagining they would eat their lunch at around midday, but later learned that the picnic was all consumed by nine-thirty am.

Nose out of joint
After watching Butlin's Holiday Camp commercials and convinced there would be plenty of entertainment and excitement, Lesley persuaded us to take her to the Pwhelli Camp. Strangely enough, I had visited this camp when it was a military training establishment during WWII and had driven a Staff Officer there from Market Drayton.

The food was very good and if you were still hungry they brought you a whole second meal. But the high spot of the holiday was when we went to see the glass-sided swimming pool where one could watch the swimmers moving underwater. I approached this interesting feature with a bit too much enthusiasm and immediately gave my nose a painful bang; I had been focusing on the inner glass wall but the outer one was at least two feet closer to me. I staggered back, wondering what had hit me and caused me to see stars. I became an object of great merriment to Cliff and Lesley and, by the time my ruffled feathers were back in place, we saw other people approaching the pool and, sure enough, they did the same!

Small earthquake – big freeze

The year we moved to our next house, Cliff had been so busy that we did not have a summer holiday and instead went to the island of Rhodes for Christmas.

It was surprisingly cold but full of interesting antiquities; we walked along the wide wall that fortified the capital, from where we could look down over the whole city.

Walking through the streets, we saw houses where the Crusaders had established their quarters and which had their personal insignia carved in stone above the doorways. We also drove to the sites of ancient Roman dwellings where we could see immaculate ceramic pipework, similar to ours today. In the countryside we passed charming Turkish villages, where the houses were painted in a variety of pastel colours.

During our stay, a small earthquake announced itself one night, by rattling the bedside table across the bedroom floor, adding a bit of excitement to the holiday.

It was here that we met a Dutch couple with whom we reminisced about WWII and our respective experiences. The wife told us that her father had been one of the leaders of the Dutch underground resistance, had been captured by the Germans but was rescued and brought to England. Here he was kept till the end of the war, under suspicion that he could have been a double agent. When he returned to Holland he was able to clear his name.

To our amazement, after they left, a huge bouquet of carnations was delivered to our room with the message: "Thank you, you RAF people". It was heartrending that they should thank us after all they had suffered.

When we got back to the UK, the country was in the grip of a major freeze. Our car engine was a solid block of ice, so we returned to Bristol by train and, as I got out of the carriage, my precious and much travelled bottle of duty free whisky fell through the paper bag and smashed. Welcome home!

Chapter 7

Angling for pleasure

Retirement of the small ball

Despite being expected to play golf from the age of eleven, I did not start to enjoy the game until handsome young men gave it a whole new slant; then the young men went to war and I did not play golf again until I was married, when my husband was delighted to discover that I knew *how* to play. I really did try to enjoy it and continued to play for several years but it was always a struggle.

The final time I played was with Cliff at Parkstone, near Bournemouth; it was a very tough course and almost at the end of the round I socked the ball really hard to get it up the hill that confronted me. It fell on the brow, hesitated for a moment and then gradually started to roll back till it reached the very spot at my feet where I had just hit it with all my might! I looked at the offending sphere for a second or two, then bent down, picked it up and put it in my pocket. I never played golf again.

So that is why Cliff taught me spinning and fly-fishing and I never looked back; I could just rest under a tree and enjoy the beautiful countryside, whenever. I wanted, without spoiling anyone else's game. In Spring, there were snowdrops, primroses, wild cherry trees, and bluebells and, in autumn, blackberries, mushrooms, hazel nuts and sloes from which we made sloe gin.

The challenge of learning how to fish
With great patience, Cliff demonstrated how to spin with a metal spinner that, in the water, looks like a small minnow. When I had mastered that, including how to put the spinner where I wanted it to go and how to untangle the nylon line a few thousand times, I was ready to graduate to fly fishing.

Well, there is the scene and here are some of the potential pitfalls.

Firstly, do not thump about on the bank in heavy waders. The nearby fish will leave their favourite lie and go for a daytrip and may not return until who knows when.

The second thing is to become totally proficient at tying the various knots required for success, particularly where nylon and similarly slippery materials are involved, otherwise the fish you think you have hooked may take off upstream with just your cast and fly. Not good for his survival, unless he works out how rid himself of the hook, a knack shown to me by one of the salmon I failed to land.

The next step is learning how to cast and, by experience, not to land the fly between one's shoulder blades, firmly hooked into your Fairisle jumper, the overhead tree, the bush on your left, the willow on the opposite bank or into your finger, up past the barb, as I once did.

Despite these technical hurdles, it is a totally artistic occupation with the line and the fly sweeping through the air in ever increasing distances, until one is ready to let it land delicately onto the surface of the water, just where a fish is likely to be resting... or not. Perfecting this step is enthralling and beautiful to watch. It takes a great deal of concentration and practice but is so engaging that one does not necessarily need to catch fish, and indeed, it was many years before I caught a salmon and a few more before I caught a salmon with a fly.

And that is how I started angling, taking to it like a duck to water. Yes, fishing was truly *my* game and I got quite good at it.

Three fishy tales

Our first fishing holiday and my introduction to the sport, was at Llanwrtyd Wells in mid Wales. In the grounds of the hotel where we stayed, was a small lake and on Bank Holidays, residents of the village would come to picnic, take boats on the lake, and fish. I watched two men seating two ladies in the back of a skiff, then lowering the boat, stern first into the water, with the ladies in it. Suddenly there were loud screams and the two ladies were up to their waists in water as the skiff pushed down into the lake at an acute angle. The flustered menfolk quickly hauled the boat out, and I did not wait to hear the ensuing reproaches, presumably in Welsh.

The cowering brother
While staying at this hotel, we talked with two brothers who were also fishermen. One of them, who was truly scared of cows, was going fishing with his brother on a particularly dark night. The nervous one had his hand on the shoulder of his brother's leather jacket and presently they came to a stile; the brave brother climbed over and walked on a few paces. The nervous one, taking a

little longer to see his way in the dark, followed and put his hand back on his brother's shoulder. He asked if they were nearly there and got no reply. He thought his brother's shoulder was rather warm and realised, to his horror, that he had his hand on the rump of a cow.

The old rope trick
These same brothers were spinning for salmon one day and felt they had chosen a good spot on the river bank; however, they had been angling there some time without success.

Presently two lads from the village came to watch them and asked if the brothers would mind if they took a salmon out of the river where they were standing. Fed up with their own lack of success they said, "Go ahead – and good luck!"

One lad put a rope down the right sleeve of his friend's coat and attached a running noose to the end of it. Then he stepped back further into the field, holding the other end of the rope and when his friend shouted it meant the loop was in position over the tail of a salmon. On hearing the shout, the man holding the end of the rope gave a fearsome tug on it, and the salmon, caught in the noose, flew up over their heads and into the field, to the astonishment of the anglers. The poachers then asked if they could take another salmon and the anglers agreed, imagining they couldn't possibly find a second one. They watched open-mouthed as yet another salmon flew up into the field. The poachers thanked the anglers politely and said "We've left one there for you!"

Tales of the unexpected

From my many years of enjoying the fresh air and beautiful surroundings, I treasure two particular moments beside the river.

The Heron
One evening, I was sitting peacefully on a small grassy island, munching a sandwich and waiting for the light to fade, so I could start fishing for sea trout. Suddenly there was a great fluttering of wings and a large heron landed about two yards away from me. I kept very still and we sat in quiet companionship, contemplating the fishing possibilities; he clearly didn't think much of them, for ten minutes later he flew off.

The Fox
The second joy was when I was fishing friends' water in North Devon. The banks were high and the water was low and every fish in that stretch had an ideal view of me waving my arms about; so I gave up and sat down for a rest on a fallen tree.

Presently I heard the sound of the local hunt in full cry — probably about a mile away across the river. At that moment I caught sight of something moving to my right; I turned slowly and saw a handsome fox, who sat a few yards away, his ears pricked — listening, like me, to the sounds of the hunt. We sat there, at ease with each other, until he felt it was prudent to leave, when he loped off into the woods on the hill behind us. It was a blank fishing day but a very treasured memory.

Mistaken identity
When we were on a fishing holiday in Devon, we stayed

in an hotel where an artist friend of ours and his wife were also guests. Lesley was about nine and we thought she might enjoy trying to fish this river, as it was so full of small fish that, with three flies on my line, I once hooked three little fish at one cast and returned them to their home.

Lesley was casting across the water with a fair degree of accuracy when she suddenly shouted, "Mummy, I've caught a fish!" I ran back to help her as she was pulling on the line and a little brown head seemed to appear; I soon realised that her hook was caught in the brown weed that sometimes coats rocks and I had to break the news to her that this was not a fish; seriously disappointed she said, "Oh, I thought I had caught a kipper".

Later the artist gave her a charming watercolour painting of a little girl with a pigtail catching a big fish. It was titled Lesley and Spotted Dick.

Take a bowl of good stock
While the salmon fishing was off-season, Cliff had the idea that we could go pike fishing from a boat on Cheddar Reservoir. One January day we ventured out, though it was so cold that as the water ran down the rod, icicles formed and hung from the rings and the wind was so strong that it if / was rowing, we stayed exactly where we were! At around three o'clock, Cliff caught a six-pound pike, which he despatched neatly with a hammer blow to the head before it could bite his leg.

An hour or so later, longing to get warm, we took the catch home. As we were going to play bridge with friends that evening, Cliff went to fetch the baby-sitter and I consulted my copy of Mrs. Beeton, where I found a pike recipe which began "take a bowl of good stock…"

As I carried the bowl from the larder into the kitchen, the fish, which was on the draining board, rose head and tail and slammed down again. It was such a shock that I threw the stock in the air and stood gazing at this gallant fish, who we thought had received the coup de grace three hours earlier, knowing that there was no way I could kill it.

After I had cleared up the mess and Cliff had come home, I had to confess that I couldn't kill the pike and neither of us fancied eating it. Cliff had the mischievous idea of taking the fish to our friends and during the evening he somehow managed to slip it into their kitchen sink, where it remained undiscovered until after we'd left.

We arrived home to find the phone ringing and a very angry wife telling us to come and collect the fish at once! We did not comply with this request and learned later it had been put in their dustbin. Remarkably, the friendship survived this fishy business.

The West Wales Idyll

Cliff's saw an advertisement in his fishing magazine, for farm holidays, which included salmon and trout fishing.

The farm was Gilfachwen in Llandyssul, West Wales, on the river Teifi and we went there with the two children and faithful Florrie to cook for us, as I wanted to spend the time becoming more proficient at fishing. We loved it so much we spent three happy holidays there; Sally, the farmer's wife, was especially welcoming and would have cakes, fresh from the oven, waiting for us.

The Forbidden Word
When we first started fishing the Teifi, Tom, Sally's husband, would come in every evening to ask whether we'd caught any sea trout. Tom had explained to us that a delicate touch was needed to hook and land sewin (the Welsh name for sea trout) because they had very soft mouths and the fly was easily torn away when they leaped.

Each evening we'd bemoan our lack of success and he would say "Oh damn, they're buggers". The girls knew this was a forbidden word and would wait for it eagerly, their two heads nodding in unison, delighted to hear that naughty word night after night.

An unexpected catch
One pitch-black night, Cliff was fishing Llain Fain (narrow meadow). As he was building up the casting distance, moving the rod backwards and forwards and extending the line with each cast, he was amazed to hear the reel running out of control. Instinctively he tried to wind in the line but soon realised he had hooked a cow and that the offended creature had broken the nylon cast, leaving the fly embedded in its hide.

Cliff went to the Bercoed farmhouse and confessed shamefacedly to Farmer Davies; misunderstanding the reason for his confession, the farmer said, "Don't you worry Mr. Farrow, you shall have your fly back in the morning." And indeed he did.

Ill met by moonlight

We invited married friends to stay with us at Gilfachwen and during their visit; we all went for drinks with other friends who lived in a bungalow in the small nearby wood.

The path to their home was rather rustic and difficult to negotiate in the dark, but all four of us arrived safely with a bottle of whisky and enjoyed a convivial evening. When we left, Cliff and the wife went on ahead, and I followed a little unsteadily. Wondering where the husband was, I turned round and saw, on the horizon, the most gigantic, golden harvest moon. Silhouetted against it was the husband, privately, as he thought, relieving himself. Every detail was precisely outlined, even the black tracery of the beautiful but unfortunate fern at his feet.

Perhaps fuelled by the alcohol intake, I was seized with uncontrollable laughter and experienced even more difficulty negotiating the path than I had on the outward journey. Unfortunately, I couldn't speak coherently enough to explain what I was laughing about as Cliff helped me home, muttering under his breath "I can't stand drunken women".

Salmon hatchery

When we first fished the Teifi, we visited a salmon hatchery on a small tributary, which led to a natural spawning area. The point of this exercise was to hatch the eggs out of the reach of predators. We were shown the trap in the stream from which salmon could be taken out. If it was a female fish, it was stripped of eggs over a container and then returned to the stream. As soon as a male salmon was trapped it was similarly stripped over the same container, fertilising the eggs; the male was then also returned to the water. As the eggs hatched, tiny fish, known as fry, were kept in stacked trays with water constantly running through them. They were carefully tended and moved from tray to tray as they grew larger; any dead fish were removed. Once they were large enough to survive alone, they were released back into the stream.

Cliff would assist in the study of the salmon and every time we caught one he would send some scales to the government fisheries laboratory for analysis. I understood that the number of rings on a scale, would indicate the number of years the fish had survived, returned to the sea and come back to its native river. A very high percentage of salmon hatched do not survive. Sadly the hatchery was closed, however Cliff still kept in touch with the fishery services.

For those who are interested, *Salar the Salmon* by Henry Williamson, is an excellent book, which details the lifecycle of the salmon. The story is told from Salar's viewpoint and outlines his battle to survive by avoiding his many predators, including seals in the estuaries, heron, otters, commercially licensed fishermen netting across the mouth of the river and sporting fishermen.

The bull and the gate
When fishing, we were always mindful of closing gates to keep the farmers' stock secure. One day, when I'd finished fishing, with our border collie, Teifi, at my heels, I walked across the field to the gate, which I found lying on the ground. Out of habit I picked it up and, using the available baling twine attached to it, fixed the gate in the upright, closed position.

I turned round to retrieve my fly rod and found myself confronted by the biggest bull I'd ever seen, just five yards in front of me. I had not heard a single sound as he came round the corner to where I was busy doing my good works. Fenced in as a result of my own handiwork, I called Teifi to heel and was grateful for the time I had spent training him. The bull and I eye-balled each other in heavy silence.

With infinitely slow movements I grasped my rod and inched backwards towards a clump of sturdy bushes, keeping steady eye contact with this great creature. Once concealed by the bushes, I peeped back to see what he was doing. With a look of the utmost disdain on his noble face, he approached the upright gate, fixed his horn into the knot I had so carefully tied, broke the twine, and let the gate fall to the ground, exactly where it had been when I'd first entered his domain.

Ones that got away

Cliff and I and a client called John, were all fishing a stretch of the Teifi called Blackpool Flats, which extended along two fields. Cliff was upstream in the second field, I was at the top of the first field and John was half way down the first field.

Almost immediately, I got into a salmon. I brought it to the bank but as the river was very low, the fish was out of my reach; so I called Cliff, who came running down to tail it for me; he had to lie full length in order to reach the fish and as he was doing so the hook on the minnow broke off and the fish was gone.

The water looked beautiful so, undeterred, I walked

downstream a few yards, cast again and got into another salmon. This time I was determined to land the fish so, holding the rod up high and keeping the tension of the line tight in my fingers, I started to run downstream towards a little beach, where John shouted "I'll land it for you". Unfortunately, a mean bramble from the river bank had rooted itself in a loop across my path and as I ran, still holding my rod aloft, I caught my wader in this snare and fell, losing my grip on the rod. And that was that…when I picked myself up, my second salmon had gone.

Undaunted, I moved a few yards further downstream and amazingly, got into a third salmon. This time, John was at my side assuring me he would land it. We reached the beach with the fish still hooked, and this time it looked like a certainty… However, there was a clump of wild iris at the water's edge and the fish was almost mine when he made a rush for the irises and, in a skilful manoeuvre, deposited the treble hook from his mouth straight into the clump and was gone. Losing three salmon in one day was a bitter blow.

I walked dejectedly to the top field and started fishing again. Within five minutes, I had caught a fourth salmon and brought it to the bank but it was in exceedingly poor condition and I released it to die in its native waters. It was a disappointing day for the men, who did not get into one fish but an exciting day for me and the salmon, all of whom survived.

Men 0, Woman 1, Salmon 3

The great escape
I was standing on the narrow path at Forest Pool, watching Cliff spinning for salmon. It was a brilliant, sunny day and I thought our chances of catching any fish were

low. I was wrong! Cliff hooked a salmon in the fast, glistening water, brought it successfully to the tailer, and gave the coup de grace to this fine fourteen-pounder.

As salmon sometimes travel upstream to their breeding grounds in pairs, I turned and cast my blue and silver minnow in a similar part of the water to where Cliff had been successful; it was immediately snatched and taken downstream. As I was reeling the fish back up the fast water, it suddenly reared up, head and tail, lashed at the cast with its tail, freed the minnow from its mouth and was gone. I was astonished as I said a silent goodbye to such a gallant and ingenious creature.

Man 1, Woman 0, Salmon 1

All about bait

Winter wizardry
During the winter months, Clifford would tie all the flies we needed for the next fishing season, in different styles and sizes to tempt the appetites of salmon, sea trout and trout. He had a beautiful, colour-illustrated encyclopaedia of salmon and trout flies, each individually named; this was accompanied by a box full of feathers of every hue and other materials needed to make realistic representations of each fly. In spite of the fact that I did delicate embroidery, I was totally defeated in trying to emulate my husband's nimble, fly-tying skills; this was all the more galling since his fingers and thumbs were very much larger than mine. His limitless patience was admirable.

The Bloody Butcher
I was fly-fishing on the Teifi one night and decided to go into the next field, which involved crossing a small, rather overgrown footbridge. Having a fly at the end of my cast

and also a dropper with a fly on it, I decided the safest way to get the delicate rod through the greenery without damage, was to fix the tail fly into the cork handle and throw the rod gently, tip first, into the field.

Unfortunately, I had not reckoned on the dropper flying loose; the second fly sank itself speedily into my finger, well past the barb of the hook. Thus disabled from even holding the rod, I cut the dropper lose from the cast and went in search of Cliff, who drove me to an accommodating doctor.

As he watched the doctor numb my finger and cut free the offending fly, Cliff muttered "Bloody Butcher". The doctor raised his head sharply and said "I BEG your pardon!" Cliff explained that this was the given name for the fly he had just liberated, and calm was restored. Knowing Cliff's lively sense of humour, my guess was that this was an irresistible opportunity for mischievousness.

Heads you lose, tails you win
When the river was too coloured to fish with fly or spinner one could fish with a worm. The large lob-worms were quite expensive to buy but luckily we met a cheery fellow in a fishing hotel in Scotland and he taught us how to catch worms at night; he took us out to the large hotel lawn, carrying a shaded torch and explained the drill.

The first thing to know is that the worm stretches out in the dewy grass but as a means of swift escape, keeps its tail tucked in its hole. When danger looms, such as a heavy footfall, the worm disappears back into the hole as fast as a released, stretched elastic band.

As our friend had had a few, he demonstrated this phenomenon right away with uncontrolled footsteps, and there was suddenly not a single worm in sight. When they eventually returned, he showed us that the knack was to grab the worm near the tail end, thus thwarting the re-entry of the rest of its body into the hole. They move so fast that trying to catch them by the head will invariably fail.

We thanked him profusely, took him into the bar for another drink, borrowed his torch and tried out this new money-saving exercise. By George, we did it and did it for years at home afterwards too. The neighbours never complained about our strange, nocturnal habits and our compost heaps became a worm nursery of consequence; little shouts of "missed it, dammit" were occasionally heard but we both became pretty adept and carried our harvest down to the cottage as needed, where it resided in a large zinc bath, full of good soil and moss in the back garden.

Against all odds
I was fishing one day on Blackpool Flats, and Bob, a genial member of our angling syndicate, who was comparatively new to fishing, was spinning Blackpool a couple of fields away. Suddenly I became aware of terrific splashing, shouting and swearing which went on for some minutes and then it went quiet. Slightly alarmed I hurried down to Blackpool, where I found Bob, shaking all over. My relief at finding he was alright turned to amazement as he showed me the enormous salmon, which turned out to weigh thirty pounds, that he had safely landed alone. Cliff and I took Bob and the fish back to the cottage and gave

Bob a double brandy to celebrate his triumph and restore his shattered nerves.

Anniversary gifts
By far the most exciting fishing day we ever had on the River Teifi, was on our twenty-second wedding anniversary, when the river was in prime condition and so were we! To my utter amazement, fishing with a spinner, I fought and landed four salmon on Blackpool Flats, and had to get help to carry them to the car.

I was both thrilled and totally exhausted as I drove back to the farm, only to find that Cliff had landed three salmon. The total catch weighed in at fifty pounds and Tom, the farmer, was so excited he called the local photographer and photographs were duly taken. What an extraordinary way to celebrate a wedding anniversary! A piece appeared in the Bristol evening newspaper the following week, announcing that Mr. and Mrs. Clifford Farrow had landed fifty pounds of salmon in one day in Wales that weekend.

Man 3, Woman 4, Salmon 0

Forty-three years later, in 2008, I returned to Llandyssul and, unannounced, called on Farmer Jeffrey Davies at Bercoed Farm near Blackpool Flats. Before I had a chance even to say hello, he rushed towards me with outstretched hand and said "You're the lady who caught four salmon in one day!

All in the same boat
A client invited us, one evening, to fish the Directors' Pool, a small reservoir south of Bristol. I took a special picnic and Cliff brought a bottle of wine. To my surprise, our host crammed all three of us into an unbelievably

small rowing boat and in no time we were all casting flies over our respective heads. The men each caught a nice trout and then it was time for supper. We ate and drank on board, enjoying the delightful surroundings, the sound of leaping trout and each other's company.

I am not noted for staying sober for long after the intake of alcohol, so, before I even had the chance to adjust my thinking from drinking to casting safely, a trout had taken my fly, which was resting lazily on top of the water. Netting the fish set me off into fits of giggles, over which I had only slight control, earning me a stern look from Cliff but not from our genial, client host. We all caught fish and after dark, rowed to the grassy landing stage which, to my joy, was alight with hundreds of glow worms – a sight I had never seen in my life before. Yes, they really were glow-worms, it wasn't the alcohol!

Chapter 8

A home from home

Top of the big hill

We so loved Llandyssul that we decided to try and buy a small cottage where we would be free to come and go any time we liked without being tied to rental periods.

Annie and I searched the neighbourhood and came to hear of a place that we could actually see from Gilfachwen, as it was on a hill across the Teifi valley. I was excited to tell Cliff when he came in from fishing and we went together to view the house and decided immediately to buy it. Just £400, cash down and Penrhiwfawr, including three acres of land, was ours.

Penrhiwfawr means top of the big hill and our cottage commanded magnificent views of the Teifi Valley. It had two and a half bedrooms, two reception rooms and a kitchen, no electricity, mains water or indoor toilet, though there was a privy in a little shed across the road. But we could see the property had potential and it was dry, bright and easy to clean.

I later understood that this was a Sundowner's cottage. By this was meant that the builder of a house could take advantage of an old law whereby if someone had gathered his friends and family together and they had managed to build the outer walls of a house and get the roof on, between sun up and sundown, they could claim three acres of land to go with the building.

We knocked down the extension, which had contained a bread oven, and rebuilt it as a kitchen plus a small bathroom and adjoining lavatory with an outside door. This meant, that at times of fine weather, one could be seated on the loo and sunbathe all at the same time.

Mains water was installed and the builder fashioned a log store and an attractive open fire with a Baxi grate for easy lighting. This fire heated the downstairs rooms and hot water but initially we had to use oil lamps and a calor gas cooker. It took a couple of years to persuade enough farmers to agree to join in a new circuit before we were able to get mains electricity installed.

There was a small cupboard alongside the fireplace from which smoke used to escape. I investigated and found there was paper stuffed in an opening from the chimney. The paper turned out to be the sheet music of the popular World War I song, *Hello, Hello, who's your lady friend?*.

When the renovation was complete, Cliff asked me what colour I would like the cottage to be painted. I said "pink" – like many cottages in Devon. But farmer, Tom, was less than impressed and commented, "that's a funny colour to paint a cottage".

There was a very sharp left hand bend in the road, just beyond the cottage and the local highways surveyor wanted to make this safer by cutting off a corner of our field. He had no funds available to pay for the piece of land, however, in exchange for it, he offered to take down our ruined barn, clear the area and lay gravel on the vacated space, which gave us three parking places. This arrangement suited both parties down to the ground.

We learned that once a week a large van, containing used furniture, came down from London to a field in a tiny hamlet called Cum Tudu (pronounced Cum Tiddy). As pieces were unloaded, people would shout out a bid and the highest bidder got the piece. We bought five beds, a dining table and chairs, a Welsh settle, and a footstool, all for £40.

Some years later we joined forces with two friends and bought the fishing rights to two miles of bank on the opposite side to that owned by Tom. By mutual agreement we arranged that we could all fish from both banks.

Current accounts

We took our friend and client Bill, his wife Joan and their son to the cottage for a few days. Joan, her son and I were fishing Dan Graig Pool and, by exceedingly good fortune, while I was showing Joan where to land a spinner, I hooked a salmon. The current was helping us and, as I brought the fish to the bank, I asked the boy if he would like to tail it for me. A tailer is a wire running noose, which one places around the tail and slightly up the body of a hooked salmon and with a sharp upward pull the noose closes over the tail so one can pull the fish onto the bank. It's a delicate action, as the noose mustn't touch the flanks of the salmon before you're ready to land it, or you may lose it. The boy did it to perfection and we were all excited to see a beautiful, eleven-pound salmon secured on the bank.

During their stay, we loaned Bill my salmon rod and I took his lighter rod in exchange. We all went to Blackpool, which was the best holding pool (rest place for many salmon on their journey upstream). To give our guests plenty of room to fish, I decided to cross the river and fish upstream out of their way. To do this, I had to cross two small, grassy islands and negotiate the main flow of the river between them, which I was well accustomed to doing. But this time I put one wader in the stream, went to put the second wader down and the current neatly removed the stones from under my first foot; I was swept away and found myself sailing down the river feet first.

The first thought that came to my mind was that even if rigor mortis set in, I must not let go of the client's rod and I held it above water level the whole time, in view of Bill and Joan. Happily the swiftness and direction of the current took me into the bank downstream of where I'd started and my friends, with anxious faces, ran down to meet me. They took me home, where I stepped straight into the bath, waders and all, emptied my waders and pockets into the water and was amused to see water weed and small aquatic creatures joining me in the bath.

The river was in very fine condition for Bill and Joan's visit and because I knew she didn't have a lot of fishing experience, I put her on a fast running corner pool with a spinner and she hooked a big fish; but it flew up into the air, crashed down and immediately got off the hook. So I told her to cast in exactly the same place, which she did and hooked another fish but it too leapt up and was away. The following day I took her to Llain Fain pool where I got into a fish, which I let her play and tailed for her. It was rewarding for our guests that conditions during their visit resulted in such exciting fishing and some salmon to take home.

An uncommon Lord

On one visit to the cottage, we took our client Bob (who happened to be a Lord) and Clifford's mother, who came from an East London background. She was a bit over-whelmed, having never met a Lord before, let alone sat opposite one at the table in a modest cottage. Bob was recounting a story during supper and used the word "ain't", as in, "it ain't necessarily so". Grandma put down her knife and fork in utter astonishment and came out with this classic "What a common lord!"

This man was such a dear, understanding person and we all burst out laughing; it was a while before order was restored and we could carry on with our meal. It was typical that forthright Grandma should speak her mind right then and there.

On our weekend visits to the cottage we normally ate supper before we left home. The first time we'd taken Bob to the cottage, Clifford was to travel later so I went ahead with our guest. As a consequence, I completely forgot to provide food for supper. I stood in our little cottage kitchen abashed and confessed all to this very kindly man, offering him a humble poached egg and baked beans and a cup of tea with bread and butter. I was amused, at the end of the meal, to see Bob wiping the bread and butter around his plate with great relish.

During another of Bob's visits, we were awakened at six o' clock in the morning by a tremendous crashing and banging in the back garden. The three of us rushed out to find a small herd of cattle eating my hard won cottage garden, even the eucalyptus tree I had painstakingly grown from seed. I had to chuckle at the sight of the three of us, in our dressing gowns, herding cattle into the lane.

Bob was not only a charming guest but also a very tolerant one who was prepared to put up with being insulted by Grandma, starved by me, and expected to run around herding cows in his dressing gown at six am. I can only imagine he came back for more because he fell under the spell of the Welsh countryside and, to our delight, he did catch a salmon on the Teifi.

The consolation of the end of the fishing season was the final autumn days when the countryside turned to yellow, gold, scarlet, amber and shades in between. The numbers of floating leaves made fly-fishing tricky but the salmon ran well. Presently we packed up our little cottage, took mental pictures of all the beauty, and of the season's fish we had caught and went home, returning shortly before Christmas, to cut some branches from our wonderful holly tree and bear them back to Bristol.

Our ownership of this welcoming little cottage, in its peaceful setting, lasted twenty-five years and was greatly enjoyed by family, friends and clients.

Chapter 9

Dog Days

Dog lover

From the moment I knew what a dog was I became a lifelong dog lover and my family always had dogs. My first love was an Airedale, called Bobby, who belonged to a friend of my mother. He was considerably bigger than me but so gentle and so much fun when I played with him.

When we lived in Plymouth, Mother had a liver and white spaniel called Sarah, whose favourite game was to leave our large garden and sit in the middle of the nearby main road so, to improve her chances of survival, Mother gave her to a family who lived in the country where she would be safer.

When we moved from Plymouth to Yelverton we were given a wire-haired terrier called Whiskers. I was in my early teens, and one afternoon had just completed a round of golf with the boy next door when, as we were returning to the clubhouse, we heard a shout behind us. We went back to find a slightly irate Lady Astor accusing our terrier of picking up her ball off the eighteenth green. Sure enough, there it was in Whiskers's mouth. He had been a little way behind us and the sight of a moving ball had been just irresistible, so he had brought it to us for our next game. Apologies were given and accepted.

Scamp

When the children were quite young, Cliff brought home a cross-bred terrier puppy. He was such a rascal that he was immediately named Scamp.

Succumbing to temptation
One day I had treated myself to a daring, shocking pink, lacy nightie, which was so successful, Cliff couldn't wait for me to take it off! Unfortunately, the other male in the house also found it seductive.

Having had its first laundering, it was blowing nicely on the clothes line, with its hem just low enough for Scamp to catch in his teeth when he jumped. This was such a temptation that, in next to no time, he had the garment in shreds. We had named him well.

Reservoir dog
When Scamp was little more than a year old, we were on a picnic by a small reservoir where many birds were dipping low onto the water, catching insects. Scamp was running along the parapet, chasing the birds. However, in trying to keep close to them he would run out of parapet and go, with still-revving feet, ker-splash into the water and have to swim back to us over and over until he was tired.

While we were eating lunch, Scamp wandered off and disappeared into the long grass. As he was much shorter than the grass he lost sight of us, and we of him. Presently we saw him leap momentarily above the grass, looking for us. We then called him, but he was below grass level again and couldn't locate us.

This caper was repeated several times with him shooting vertically out of the grass in different parts of the field, without our being able to synchronise his leaps with our shouts. Finally we managed to anticipate his next appearance and, relieved to see us at last, he came running in our direction. Exhausted from his adventures that day, Scamp slept soundly all the way home.

Daphne R.I.P.

Scamp was such cheerful dog and he liked to watch me gardening. I had bought a bush, called Daphne Meserium, and was busy digging a hole in which to plant it. When it was fully installed and the earth tamped down with my gardening boot, I went on to weed the roses. When I looked back at my new acquisition, Scamp, in an attempt to copy me, had redug the hole and my namesake was lying back on the path. The poor bush went in and out the ground so many times, that it eventually lost the will to live.

Who's laughing now!

As my birthday is on 7th of November, we always had a firework party. When we moved to our first house, in Briarwood, the adjoining neighbours were a pleasant middle-aged couple, so, of course they were always invited. The only difficulty was that the husband, Bill, used to tease Scamp, whenever he saw him.

It was my practice to make a big saucepan of soup and other goodies so we could all warm up as soon as the fireworks were over. We didn't have a lot of matching china and, on one, occasion Bill got a non-matching soup bowl. We were all crowded in the kitchen and Scamp was at Bill's feet, barking like mad. Bill, as usual, taunted the dog by lifting the bowl up and down, until Cliff solemnly (though untruthfully) told him "What you don't realise, Bill, is that you have got his bowl!"

Scamp eventually grew out of his puppy mischief and was much loved. Our garden was not totally dog-proofed, so he would regularly wander off and socialise with the neighbours; at one house he would even stop off for a cup of tea. Another neighbour told me she had seen him at the top of the hill, getting on a double-decker bus! However, he never got lost and was always home in time for his supper.

Teifi

After Scamp died, at the age of eight, we both wanted another dog and the wife of one of Cliff's artists bred Border Collies. We went to see them and six little seven-inch long puppies scrambled into the room. One separated himself from the others and chose to sink his teeth into my heel. "That's the one!" shouted Cliff, and we took him home. We named him Teifi, after the river in Wales that we fished for twenty-eight years.

Tiptoe through the tulips

As we had had a dog before, there was already a dog-flap in the back door so he could roam the garden. When Teifi was half-grown and looked like an old black mat, he loved going through the flap as it made a satisfying noise.

It was spring, and my two-dozen red tulips, whose flowers I had awaited since the previous October planting, were in bloom among blue forget-me-nots. One day Teifi came in through the dog-door with a red tulip in his mouth and presented it to me. I told him "NO". So next time he came in with two tulips hanging from his jaws and looked really pleased with himself. Well, I had no joy persuading him to leave the tulips alone – and after the destruction had gone on for some time, I looked out of the window to see there were twenty-three bare stalks and one lone tulip left. In fury, I fetched a cane and slashed off the remaining bloom myself.

Bringing home the bacon
Preparing dinner, one day, I had cooked a delicious smoked gammon, which I had taken out of the saucepan and put on a plate to cool. The telephone rang and, ill-advisedly, I left it on the kitchen stool; when I returned, the gammon had disappeared and all my searches for it were in vain.

About six months later, when the French windows were open, Teifi ran in from the garden and deposited a large, stinking, earth-covered lump on the white hearthrug I'd made. It was the gammon! It smelled dreadful and so did the rug, but Teifi looked delighted to have brought me the special gift that he'd been saving up.

Out-foxed by a slippery customer
When my elegantly proper mother was staying with us, we decided to shampoo Teifi in the bath, but had not anticipated his guile. When he was covered in lather, he leapt out of the bath, and looking for the narrowest exit, ran between my mother's slender legs, ridding himself of all the lather in one sweep.

Disobedience classes
It was almost inevitable that Teifi would have chased

sheep, when we were in Wales, had he not been trained. It was well-known that farmers would shoot a dog on sight if it were chasing his sheep. So I took him to what we called, "disobedience classes", where I was taught how to handle his inbred shepherding instincts. This was achieved by putting him on a very long rope, taking him into a field of sheep and, as soon as he moved toward them and they moved away, I tugged hard on the rope causing him to tumble over and over. He was highly intelligent and eminently trainable, so in all our trips to Wales, we never had any trouble with him in respect of sheep.

Cows are curious creatures... and when I fished they would come to see who I was. This greatly inconvenienced me when fly-fishing, as my fly would travel forward and then backward towards the curious herd, and I feared it would get caught in one of the creatures. Teifi seemed to appreciate this, and discerning these beasts were not the sheep he was forbidden to round up, herded the cows at some distance from me. Having done his duty, he would often come and sit in the water beside me, keeping a keen eye open for any piscatorial activity.

Wake up ball
If there was one thing that agitated Teifi, it was golf on television. He could be fast asleep by the fire but if Cliff put on a golfing programme, the second there was the click of a cleanly hit ball, Teifi would leap to his feet and make a dash at the TV, nearly knocking it over. The armchair golfer would have to jump up smartly to rescue the set. We never fathomed whether this was an innate dislike of the game or frustration that he couldn't chase the ball, but once he had been told to sit, he would settle

down to watch the game.

Enough's enough, Jack

One winter, we went to the cottage with friends who were part of our fishing syndicate; our purpose was to take out brambles and overhanging branches to clear the way for casting during the next fishing season. Teifi, one of the best-natured dogs I have ever known, and our friends' Jack Russell and a Jack Russell puppy came along too.

It was a lovely sunny day and we stopped work to have a picnic. Teifi wanted to get a closer look at the puppy but every time he went anywhere near it, the protective older Jack Russell would understandably go for him. After a few foiled attempts to befriend the puppy, to our embarrassment, an exasperated Teifi picked up the older dog by the scruff of the neck and neatly dropped him into the river.

Our friend took to his heels, ran downstream and hauled out the swimming dog, who, to everyone's relief, was none the worse for his experience.

Gilfachwen Water
(not to scale)

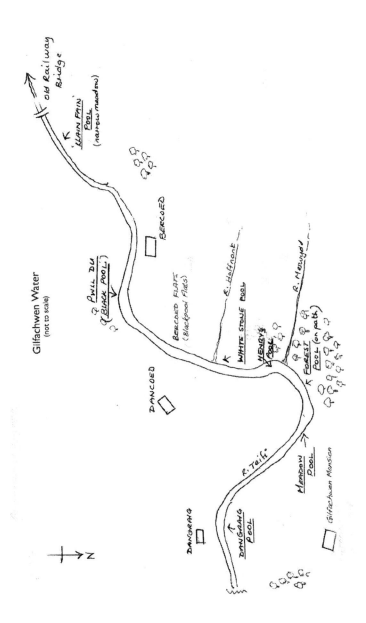

N →

R. Teifi

DANGRAIG

DANGRAIG POOL

MEADOW POOL

Gilfachwen Mansion

DANCOED

PWLL DU ('BLACK POOL')

BERCOED FLAT (Blackpool Flats)

WHITE STONE POOL

HENDY'S POOL

FOREST POOL (on path)

R. Hoffront

R. Menwyd

BERCOED

'NAIN FAIN' POOL (narrow meadow)

old Railway Bridge

1955 At this time, the other male in my life was...

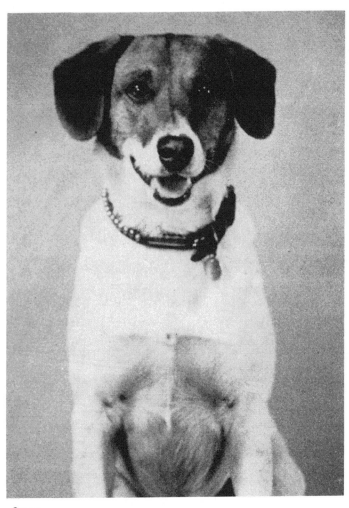

...Scamp

My two men in their country tweeds

1955 Cliff leaves me to fish Blackpool, on the Teifi at Llandyssul

1955 Spinning Blackpool, our favourite spot

Cliff fishing Blackpool flats

Salmon jumping upstream on the Teifi at Cenarth Falls

1965 Our 22nd Wedding Anniversary catch

Cliff with a 14 pound salmon

Before

1960 Penrhiwfawr - the little cottage at the top of the hill, as it was when we bought it.

and after

Teifi

1963 Cliff's mother, Elsie

Chapter 10

Bristol – the later years

Revelations for the vicar

It was a cold spring morning so I put on two thick pullovers as I went out into the garden to dig. Presently the sun came out and I grew really hot.

At that moment, Florrie shouted from the kitchen window, "The Vicar's here to see you m'am"; so I shed my wellies at the back door and raced into the sitting-room, saying, "Hello vicar". Because I was so hot, I immediately crossed my arms and started pulling off my jumper.

Mid-action, I suddenly became aware that my fingers were holding both sweaters over my head. This undoubtedly gave the Vicar a full frontal view of my belly-button, and a tantalising glimpse of my lacy bra. Arms frozen in mid-air, face burning, I struggled frantically to pull both sweaters down again, attempted to regain my composure and get the Vicar's attention back on to the reason for his visit - my daughter's confirmation.

All that glisters is not gold

Cliff was always extremely fastidious about his clothes, even having suits and jackets made to measure by a London tailor, when we couldn't really afford it. His reasoning was that clients who saw an apparently prospering man would have confidence in his abilities, and I agreed with him.

One Saturday afternoon we were sitting on the hearthrug, making toast on an open fire and I was ready with the butter and golden syrup. Cliff was wearing his favourite sports jacket. I tried unsuccessfully to open the golden syrup tin by levering the lid with a knife; "Oh give it to me!" he said, and, exerting considerable pressure on the blade, caused the lid to shoot up two feet in the air, in a fast spinning motion.

Four eyes were fixed on this phenomenon as the lid descended but neither of us predicted it would land, sticky side down, on Cliff's pristine left lapel ... but it did. We were both overtaken by gusts of laughter and just when we were beginning to recover, Cliff lifted the lid off his jacket, looked at it and stuck it back onto his lapel; now, we were helpless and had tears running down our faces.

The Oak Table

When we moved to our lovely, Edwardian family house opposite a park, our existing dining table looked too small in the spacious dining room.

I asked Cliff if I might go to a furniture auction and look for a table. He agreed as long as it cost no more than a fiver. I had never been to an auction sale before and there was a nice-looking table simply covered in china and silverware. I asked a staff member if he would bid for me; he agreed and I got it for £5. After that I went cold, as I had no idea whether the surface was damaged.

The day came when it was delivered and I was in goose bumps of apprehension. Uncovering the table I was astonished to find it was not only in prime condition but also had spare leaves which could be brought out for use by turning a handle. In addition, the whole edge of the table was carved with a design which, to my amazement, matched our chairs.

For many years this table hosted parties at Christmas, weddings and major visits as the grandchildren multiplied; but best of all, it turned out to be a marvellous ping-pong table, though the wood was so hard that the ball shot off the surface at high speed.

Cliff and Shep had established a thriving advertising agency and one day a photographer needed a picture of a staircase for an advertisement for a child gate. They decided to set up the photo shoot in our home and, to get the necessary angle, the photographer asked if he could back into the dining room. I opened the door and he stopped, open-mouthed. "Good heavens", he said, "that's my dining table!"

First Lady President
Cliff was a founder member of the Bristol Publicity Club, which met regularly to exchange views and information, and discuss developments in advertising, marketing and public relations.

I had attended a public speaking course, run by the Club, and to my great surprise, was asked if I would be willing to stand for the post of President. I agreed and was duly elected its first lady president. I presented the woman's point of view on publicity in a couple of uninspiring talks, ran a quiz, presented prizes, and enjoyed my brief tenure of the position.

On the subject of alcohol

Cliff was bemused by the fact that I was unable to take much alcohol before becoming somewhat incoherent. Hence he would explain to friends "She only has to smell the cork and she's away". After a while even I had to admit my weakness when I heard myself protesting "I'm not as drunk as thinkle peep I am".

Following a few alcoholic faux pas, he changed his tactics and explained to people that he could only take me anywhere twice, the second time to apologise.

On Christmas and Easter mornings, we would often hold a party for close friends and neighbours at which Cliff would serve his lethal champagne cocktails; he would put a small slice of orange and a sugar lump in each glass, pour in a mixture of Cointreau, brandy and orange curacao and then top up the glass with champagne. As the party progressed, he would go round refilling our glasses with the liqueur mixture from a bottle labelled "Neutraliser" in one hand and champagne in the other!

After one such party Lesley, who was about eight, came into the lounge when all the guests had left, laid down on the hearthrug and said in a slurred voice "Oh mummy you do look old!" She didn't look too good herself and we found she had been out in the kitchen sucking all the alcohol-soaked orange slices and was tight as a tick.

After many years of diligent practice, I was able to cook and present a splendid Christmas dinner for twelve, while in a state of high inebriation, and never once dropped the turkey. I did once catch it on fire but, on that occasion, it was not entirely my fault. Foil had not yet been invented and thick brown paper, well-greased, was all that was available. We had been to neighbours for Christmas drinks and when we got home, I opened the oven door, the gas flared up, the greasy paper caught fire and I found myself washing a very hot turkey under the cold tap to remove the smuts.

This was my life

My sixtieth birthday was a delightful celebration; our daughters and lots of friends were there and I made a grand buffet, as our freezer always contained plenty of smoked and fresh salmon from our Welsh fishing adventures. Cliff, as usual, circulated with his lethal champagne cocktails.

Suddenly he called for attention and everything went quiet. I then noticed he was wearing a raincoat, which I thought rather odd. He opened a large book and, mimicking the then famous TV presenter, Eamonn Andrews, he read out "Daphne Farrow... This is your life.." His lovely secretary, Jackie, approached with what appeared to be a large, black television camera of that time, which she was holding on one shoulder and directing towards me as Cliff spoke.

We both had a sharp sense of humour and our marriage was full of funny incidents. Cliff, being such a fine writer was able to take full advantage of these, so there was laugh after laugh in his script. At the end everyone cheered and I gave him a big hug before we got back to the serious business of drinking.

Our house on Redland Green, Bristol

Fulfilling my duties as first lady President of the Bristol Publicity club

From left to right, Connie, Shep, Cliff and me at the twenty-fifth anniversary celebrations of our company, Fords of Bristol.

From left to right, me, Elsie, Cliff, and friend Ann. Hanging on the wall is the embroidered sampler which celebrated the twenty-fifth anniversary of my parents' Barton Motor Company.

Epilogue

When Cliff died in 1985, his legacy to me was my two lovely daughters and my memories of a loving, humourous, industrious and witty man who helped to fill my life with laughter.

In case you are wondering... yes, we did have rows, it worked out at about one every six years. The noisiest one being at ten o' clock one evening, when Cliff came down the step-ladder in the hall and put his foot in a bucket of off-white emulsion paint, whose contents had been destined for the ceiling. The paint covered the parquet flooring and splattered the oak panelling on the walls.

Trying to repair the damage next day, I was on my knees for many hours. Overwhelmed by the task, I rang Cliff, invited him home for lunch and set on him like a virago the moment he opened the door. We had the most wonderful row, complicated by the fact that the window cleaner was gripped by our domestic drama, so, despite our moving the battlefield from room to room to avoid him, he seem determined to watch the denouement.

It ended when I said I was going home to Mother and Cliff said he would help me pack. Cliff, having had no lunch, slammed the front door and went back to the office. However, by the evening the idea of going home to Mother had lost it's appeal and we got busy gloss-painting the hall panelling. I also glossed over the idea that I could possibly live without him; I'm glad I did as we had forty-two happy years together.

1985 Cliff giving the speech at the wedding of friends. The speech was written on a very long strip of paper which he extracted from his sleeve! He died a week later.

November 2009 at Ashdown Park, on my eighty-eighth birthday

blurb.com